OF THEE I SING

The American Experiment and How It Can Still Succeed

Peter Childs

BALBOA
PRESS
A DIVISION OF HAY HOUSE

Balboa Press books may be ordered through booksellers or by contacting:
Balboa Press
A Division of Hay House
1663 Liberty Drive
Bloomington, IN 47403
www.balboapress.com
1-(877) 407-4847

Cover design by John Angus

Printed in the United States of America.

ISBN: 978-1-4525-8201-6 (sc)
ISBN: 978-1-4525-8203-0 (hc)
ISBN: 978-1-4525-8202-3 (e)

Library of Congress Control Number: 2013916354

Balboa Press rev. date: 11/26/2013

TABLE OF CONTENTS

Prologue viii

PART 1: STATE OF THE UNION 1
Population... 8
The Environment..10
Agriculture 20
Forestry 24
Health Care 26
Education...31
The Economy 35
Politics.. 54
Religion 71
Current Events..76

PART 2: THE FUTURE..81
The Fifth Kingdom 96
    What God Is 97
    What Faith is 100
    What Death Isn't...103
    Right and Wrong 106

Jesus 111
The Four Great Questions 117
    What Am I? 117
    Where Do I Come From? 123
    Where Am I Going? 123
    What's Going On? 123

Conclusion 126

THIS BOOK IS DEDICATED TO YOU

PROLOGUE

In this book I will be setting forth a number of ideas that are, shall we say, unusual by any normal standard. There will be a tendency on the part of many readers to ask "What kind of nut would say stuff like this?"; to just turn away and fail to take these ideas seriously. It's an understandable reaction, and the best way I can think of to deal with it is to try to demonstrate at the outset that I am a more or less normal person, of reasonably sound mind. Then, hopefully, the question will become "What kind of not-nut would say stuff like this?" Which I would like to think will put the emphasis on the "stuff" where it belongs rather than on the individual saying it, and which will hopefully encourage serious consideration of these ideas. I will therefore commence with a brief autobiographical sketch.

I remember being born (See what I mean?). I was horrified. I felt the way one must feel when the jail door slams; you're in, it's no longer theoretical, you have to deal with it. Why did I feel that way? Because I had an overwhelming realization that something was terribly wrong with this place; something so wrong that wrongness itself was accepted as a necessary, even a desirable condition of living. It wasn't a matter of something being wrong here or there, now and then; it was a state of affairs in which wrongness was constant and ubiquitous. It was everywhere, in an infinity of different forms, with its inevitable component of suffering. The worst of it was the fact that nearly every human being alive would accept such a state of affairs; almost nobody would question it or struggle against it. They would thus doom themselves (and each other) to a continuation of this wretched status quo. We would be functionally unable to realize that wrong is WRONG; that right is RIGHT. I rejected this entire world view from the start. I could not have been an easy child to raise.

It took me more than twenty years to realize that I remembered being born, during which time I demonstrated beyond a shadow of a doubt that I had as much capacity as anyone else for selfish, stupid, short-sighted, heartless behavior, and that I was willing to yield to those inclinations on an ongoing basis (I would like to think that I have improved since gaining the perspective that memory gave me!) In thinking about this unusual recall it has occurred to me that perhaps it's not necessarily that unusual; possibly we could all remember our birth but we've buried the memory because it's so traumatic. Virtually all of us react the same way upon entering this world; we burst into tears. We hear that this is necessary to get our lungs working, but wouldn't laughter do that just as well? Maybe if we were entering a world with nothing but beauty in it we'd laugh with delight.

In any case, I had a wonderful childhood and I've had a wonderful life, a few curveballs, sinkers, and sliders notwithstanding. My parents were loving, intelligent, honest people who were greatly esteemed by all who knew them. They loved their five children deeply (I was number two; four brothers and one long-suffering sister) and they sacrificed a great deal to see that each child had every advantage that could be reasonably provided. When I was three months old we moved from the Boston area to the country west of Concord, Massachusetts, where I spent the first seventeen years of my life in the countryside with no other houses in view, in one of the oldest houses in the nation; a ten-room farmhouse built right around the year 1700. I and my siblings played in the woods daily; it was our great good fortune to grow up in natural surroundings, and it is not surprising that two of us became environmental activists in later life, because we knew from experience how it felt to be immersed in the living works of God rather than the concrete creations of Man. And we didn't have TV. Or cell phones. Or computers. Or iPods, or iPads, or app-ads (maybe not even op-eds!). I remember that my parents were born before automobiles or airplanes came into common use, and how <u>old</u> that made them seem; how the wheel does turn!

My father was one of the most respected art dealers in this country. He had to go to work to support his family at the age of twelve when his father died; he worked in a book shop that sold fine prints, and it was there that he developed the appreciation and knowledge of fine art that led him to start the Childs Gallery in Boston, which he did right at the end of the Great Depression. He achieved his dreams with the gallery, supporting his family in comfortable security but without useless frills, sending each of his five children through as much schooling as they desired, and he also achieved a very high level of respect in the world of fine art. He was fascinated by American history, in which field he became a recognized expert, and he dealt with a large number of prints and paintings that were of historical interest. He contributed to many of the finest art collections in this country.

My father met my mother when she was director of an art museum in Fitchburg, Mass. She took on the career of housewife and made a thorough success of it in spite of the fact that she (a cum laude Radcliffe grad) had to forsake a potentially rewarding career to do so. She bore and raised five children in a secure and loving environment for which I will be forever grateful to both her and my father, especially after having been out in the world and having seen how often such an environment is denied to children. She also had an active social conscience that set a fine example for us kids; she corresponded with people like Eleanor Roosevelt and worked with the League of Women Voters and several other organizations. This had a strong effect on my later activism.

On my mother's side we were descended from at least one Mayflower ancestor (an indentured servant, as I recall; nothing particularly worth getting your nose in a tilt about). We were also direct descendants of Nathaniel Bowditch, who during the age of sail rewrote LaPlace's navigational calculations and produced Bowditch's Practical Navigator, which became the industry standard and the primer for the U.S. Navy for well over a hundred years (for all I know it may still be). This got us into the Boston Social Register, but that means very little to me; my interest has always been primarily in the ordinary folk who after all make up the vast majority of the human race. But Nathaniel Bowditch was not only greatly accomplished, he was also (more importantly to me) a fine human being.

Of much greater significance to me, on my father's side we are descended from three of the original Rhode Island settlers in Providence, one in particular whose genes I am deeply honored to carry; Roger Williams (about whom more later). Another of those Providence ancestors was Mary Dyer, who was hung by the Massachusetts Bay Colony for refusing to stop preaching Quakerism (there's a statue of her now on Boston Common where, I believe, they strung her up). So those who have borne the brunt of my activism over the last forty years can see at least a partial explanation in the character of my ancestors!

I went, after the third grade, to outstanding private schools (Fenn School and Belmont Hill) and to the excellent Oberlin College, but I was a mediocre student. I couldn't have cared less how Napoleon planned this or that battle, or how to devote one's life to business, politics, or any other specific "career"; what I wanted out of life was to understand it and to have fun. So I had my first eight motorcycles at Oberlin, and they kept me sane. I did, however, increase my understanding of how to use my mind at Oberlin; how to figure stuff out, and as far as I'm concerned, no higher function can be realistically expected from an educational institution. Yet.

It has always fascinated me that people so commonly regard logic, or rational thinking, as "dry". Since the entire cosmos is rationally arranged we can improve our understanding by following rational trains of thought. We commonly say "I didn't know (this or that), so I asked myself..." Hold it right there. We asked who? The person who didn't know, and by thinking properly we got the answer! Dry? I don't think so; how much better off we'd be if we all learned the method, the joy, and the potential of critical thinking, which is in such dreadfully short supply these days on planet Earth.

After college I had no plans and certainly no desire to chain myself to any "job". After doing a six month stint on active duty with the Army National Guard I discovered that I could take my guitar and banjo, which I loved, and actually get paid to pick and sing a few folk songs in the Cambridge and Boston area coffeehouses, which are still my favorite venues; no booze, and people came because they knew you, liked you, and understood what you were doing. This furnished me with enough money to survive on and I quickly realized that I could have an enormous amount of fun with very little expense. I traveled around from coffee house to coffee house, eventually driving an almost immaculate 1941 Cadillac hearse (stick shift, 35,000 original miles; two hundred bucks straight from the parlor) from Boston to Santa Monica, following the entire length of Route 66 when that was still possible, accompanied by a college classmate (Will Svanoe, who later became well known as a member of the Rooftop Singers) and with the songs of Woody Guthrie ringing in my heart. I fell in love immediately with California and settled for a time in Berkeley, which was a wonderful place to be in 1961. I puttered around town and many of the surrounding areas on my motorscooter (I sold the ten-mile-per-gallon hearse to some delighted surfers), ate lots of hamburger-and-veggie omelets and, after sleeping far too long on another college classmate's floor (bless you, Mayne!), shared a wonderful large semi-basement apartment with a friend at a cost of twenty dollars a month, which I covered by giving one lesson and playing one gig a week. The rest of my time was my own; I was one happy camper, I can assure you. I put a lot of miles on that scooter, which got about a million miles per gallon.

In 1963 I joined a trio (the Knob Lick Upper Ten Thousand) and travelled around the country for a year and a half, during which time we recorded two albums for Mercury Records and had so many good times that I can hardly remember them. OK, I'll explain the name. The group had formed before I met them; they named it by putting a finger on the map and choosing the place name that the finger touched, which happened to be Knob Lick, Kentucky (named, like several other southern towns, for natural salt licks in the soil). The Upper Ten Thousand was a German cognate for our "Upper Four Hundred", so we were ostensibly the Upper Crust of Knob Lick.

We spent one particularly memorable night in Knob Lick. We were traveling south to do a gig in Florida and decided that since we were going quite near Knob Lick we should stop in. It was a tiny settlement with one general store, into which we marched and announced that we played music and had named ourselves after their town. They were delighted; the phone in the store was put to immediate use and we soon had a fascinating and varied bunch of local folk stomping and hollering around while we played and sang. A couple of very colorful characters invited us over to their place well after dark, and they turned out to be bootleggers. Lights would come up the road every hour or so; the man of the house would head out to the barn, pull a stone from the foundation, and deal out some moonshine. Plenty of which he brought back into the house; all I can say about that is that I prefer milder stuff. A memorable visit, not least because in Knob Lick I bought, for a hundred and fifteen dollars, a 1941 Gibson rosewood J-200 guitar, one of only four I've ever seen and which I eventually sold for twenty-five thousand dollars.

The group broke up in 1964 and I started living in Greenwich Village (with the now justly renowned singer-songwriter John Sebastian, who snagged us an extremely desirable apartment by happening to speak the exact Italian dialect that the landlord spoke) and doing studio and accompanist work. A note that will be reflected in the ensuing pages: at that wonderful time and place some of us began referring to ourselves as "hippies" because we had discovered that we could get "hipper", which is to say that we could acquire understanding, not just knowledge. It was one of the early manifestations of the spiritual growth that lay at the heart of the Sixties, in spite of the fact that the term caught on and was eventually applied to every stray teeny-bopper who landed in Haight-Ashbury (Lord love 'em). To us "hippie" was and is a spiritual term.

One of the most memorable highlights of that time was a seven-week trip I made as guitarist for the great singer (and human being) Odetta to Europe, Scandinavia, and Africa, the last being especially unforgettable. Odetta was black; a sister from America, traditionally built, and the young politicians who were preparing to take over Nigeria fell all over each other to get next to her. She was also a person of extraordinary presence and personal power, and a wonderful artist with whom it was a pleasure to play.

I'll tell you a story about Odetta; about what I call her "presence". When we came back from that tour we landed in Los Angeles and headed through customs. They were opening and checking the contents of every bag, which was of substantial concern to me because (I hate to admit to such stupidity) I had about a pound of pot rolled up in socks in my suitcase. Maybe half of it was Nigerian black ganja that I'd gotten through the driver of our car in Lagos, some of the most wonderful herb that's ever crossed my lips (several of my old friends will remember that ganja!) and worth a certain amount of risk. But not that much; my heart almost stopped. I was certain that I was going down, far and fast. But Odetta was right in front of me in line. She knew that I was carrying pot (although she didn't smoke it). The customs guy opened my suitcase and reached out to grab my stuff, and Odetta simply *put something* on the man; I can't describe it any other way. I don't think she said a word. But his hand stopped in mid-air; he closed my bag and passed it through. I owe you, Detta, I owe you... So she was a tremendously powerful person (she passed on a couple of years ago), but my primary image of her will always be the radiant face of a sixteen year old girl, illuminated by flashes of lightning while looking at the rain splashing on the cobblestones below our hotel in Brussels.

I went on to record with a variety of artists from Peter, Paul, and Mary to Linda Ronstadt. Arguably the finest artist I ever worked with was my friend Fred Neil, an absolutely amazing singer who eschewed the limelight, which he could afford to do since one of his songs ("Everybody's Talking") made a pile of money (several others did okay, too). Volumes could and surely will be written about him; he's starting to get the attention that he sought so hard to avoid when he was alive, and which he so richly deserves. When I say he avoided attention, I mean seriously; for example, Johnny Cash tried to get him to go on his TV show but Fred wouldn't do it, and I won't soon forget being backstage at The Band's "Last Waltz", guitar in hand, with The Band (and me) begging him to come out and perform; no dice.

But he was a magical artist and person. I have had two women tell me that they gave birth to their children to his singing, and that doesn't surprise me at all. There was something about that magnificent voice that made you feel that no matter how bad things happened to be, they would turn out all right. To me he will always be, in the words of one of his songs, a "lost child in a world of sorrow". He couldn't stand to see anyone, indeed any creature, in pain (listen to his song "Dolphins"). Rest in peace, dear friend; those of us who loved you were blessed to share this life with you. We'll catch up with you later.

At the end of the sixties I was living in Topanga Canyon (outside of Los Angeles); one of several special places in which I've been fortunate to spend time. I lived on property belonging to two remarkable people, Mime and Henry Smith. Henry is a full-blood Chippewa and Mime utterly defies description. Let's just say that she's the only person I've ever given a bag of the good herb to on their eightieth birthday, and well received it was, too. I can hear her now: "Mister Childs! Mister Childs! The fucking pigs were calling my name with the bullhorn from their helicopter!" What can I say? Ask anyone in Topanga Canyon about Mime (who passed on last year) and Henry, two of the finest human beings it has been my good fortune to know; many a young person in need was taken in by them; the Canyon and its environment had no better friends. They were true guardians of "the land and the life". For a few years we had a group of maybe a dozen people there that we used to call "The Insane Asylum", and with good reason. I was "The Bishop" of the Insane Asylum; an honorable position if ever I held one. Fine times. Fine times. Too many stories; they need a book of their own.

In 1969 a lovely young woman moved in right below my cabin on Mime and Henry's land with her two children from a recently-terminated marriage and the rest, as they say, is history. Sherry, Tyce, Tina, and I moved in 1971 to Northern California, where we bought forty acres in the mountains where we can still see thirty-five miles of mountains and only four lights at night. Sherry designed a charming little house, I built it, and we've lived there ever since.

The house was illegal (and thus subject to being bulldozed) owing to the fact that it wasn't up to code; for example, my electrical outlets weren't spaced right (They didn't exist; we were and are off the grid. We used kerosene lanterns for the first fourteen years, until solar panels came along). When I suggested that of course this wouldn't apply to me the nice guys in the Building Department said "Sorry, but it's the law." The not so nice guys said "Tough luck, buddy; it's the law." (Not once, ever, has one of them said anything like "You know, you don't hire us to hassle you; you hire us to help you. Let's go together to the Board of Supervisors or to Sacramento and see if we can get some flexibility built into these regulations.") Being as I didn't care for the fact that my house could be "abated" I plunged into the world of housing activism (fighting county government) that still has me in its tentacles thirty-five years later. Perhaps the most significant result, at least for me and about three hundred other people to date, was our creation of the Alternative Owner-Builder Ordinance, which legalized our homes under much more realistic and humane rules than the standard Uniform Building Code. I have AOB permit #1 on my wall, and it gives me great satisfaction, particularly when I remember how much work it took to get the thing actually approved and passed.

Then our local three hundred acre stand of virgin Douglas Fir was threatened with logging, so into the wonderful world of forestry activism I dove. We saved Gilham Butte (along with five other beautiful areas), although we had to do it twice to make it stick, and a few years ago I had the great pleasure of taking my granddaughter for her first walk through that still-virgin forest.

Then there were the redwoods, and the whole "Redwood Summer" of protest and demonstrations sparkplugged by Judy Bari and Darryl Cherney, who were car-bombed for their efforts. Judy survived with terrible injuries and Darryl miraculously escaped relatively unscathed; a long story but they eventually sued the FBI, who had behaved despicably (and who continue to do so; at first they charged Judi and Darryl with knowingly carrying the bomb; they never tried to find the real bomber, and they are still attempting to withhold vital evidence), and won over four million dollars. Darryl has just come out with a movie about it: "Who Bombed Judi Bari?" Well worth seeing.

During Redwood Summer over a thousand people were arrested in the biggest demonstration (over four hundred in a smaller one), which helped save the largest remaining privately owned grove of virgin redwoods. I was one of seven of those arrested who eventually went to trial, which I was eager to do because I wanted to (and did) enter into the record a defense of "moral necessity". Not that it means a great deal to anyone but me, but you know; one of those things. My granddaughter can pass on the photo of Bompa being led away in handcuffs.

We started our own radio station down in town, KMUD; it's a gem. Still going after all these years, and a model of what responsible media are supposed to be. I served on the original KMUD Board of Directors for six years, and I did their first talk show for two and a half years. It was my good fortune to write the station motto, "To entertain, to inform, to inspire", which is exactly what this wonderful little station has done for twenty-five years. I also served on five other non-profit boards over the years, in efforts ranging from saving alerce trees in Chile (remarkably like redwoods) to our alternative health center, to helping people with all sorts of needs that they were unable to deal with; that kind of thing.

So it's been interesting and rewarding, with plenty to do apart from the multiple responsibilities of home and hearth off the grid (you don't want to know what thirty-five years of hand-splitting firewood has done to my shoulders!). But the core of it all for me has been, all my life, to find out what it was all about. I always wanted to know the answers to the Four Great Questions: What am I? Where do I come from? Where am I going? What's going on? Very early in this life I discovered that almost nobody even asks these questions, for a very good reason; everybody (every "authority") tells us that we cannot know the answers to such questions, so why waste life's precious time on an impossible task? But of course we are what we are, we come from where we come from, we're going where we're going, and things are what they are. The real question is whether or not we can actually understand these things. And in spite of the fact that we almost universally think we can't, every Sunday large numbers of us go to a special building for the express purpose of glorifying an individual who told us that we can indeed discover the answers to all these questions, together with how to go about it and a great deal of what we can expect to find if and when we seek. On Monday we forget all about it and go back to business as usual. Then, lacking in such basic information, we blunder along with exponentially increasing power to affect each other and the environment until we find ourselves in the desperate situation that we're in today. We just don't know what we're doing. No wonder the most realistic thing to do seems to be to make as much money as possible to cushion the shocks of life and, hopefully, to be happy. But simple material accumulation is not what we're here for, and the time has come for us to awaken to a whole new octave of being. We're being forced by the consequences of doing so wrong for so long to now seriously ask what is right. More on this to come, but one thought to hold: what if we do finally get it right? What will life be like then?

I was naive enough to think that in college, at last, I would actually get "higher education"; in other words that I would find teachers who could enlighten me about the really important things in life. That was unfair for me to expect, of course, and I can only blame my disappointment on my unrealistic expectations. But I was indeed disappointed, so it was with great excitement that I, along with about five of my friends in Cambridge in the mid-sixties, got together with Isabel Hickey, an astonishingly expert astrologer and far more important, a person of great spiritual awareness who took us under her wing every Friday night and told us the things I'd always longed to hear. She was the real thing; the first thing she told us was "Dears, don't take anything I say to be true just because you like the sound of it or because you like me. Your job is to take these ideas into the laboratory of your own lives and do the experiments that will demonstrate to you their truth or falsehood. I will tell you the truth as I believe it to be, based on the life I have lived; that's all I can or should do." Izzy was my guru, and a high privilege it was to have her as a teacher. Not only did she accurately outline what would happen in the world and in this nation since that time, she put it in context with humanity's past and with its future.

One thing leads to another; over the years a great many experiences together with quite a lot of study and thought have led me to the conclusions that I now feel obliged, in this time of desperate need, to set forth while there's still time. So let's have at it, with the same caveat that my dear teacher presented us with: don't take anything I say to be true just because you like the way it sounds (should that be the case!). Go out and, in Izzy's words, do the experiments in the laboratory of your own life, that demonstrate to you the truth or falsehood of these ideas. Question them; feel them out and think them through for yourself; truth is useful to us only when we, as individuals, really get it.

PART ONE

STATE OF THE UNION

"The preservation of the sacred fire of liberty…(is) justly considered as staked deeply, perhaps as finally, upon the experiment entrusted to the hands of the American people." (George Washington)

What I propose to set forth is that 1) we have brought the American Experiment to near-extinction because we have failed to understand it, and 2) the importance of that experiment is vastly greater than most of us have ever imagined. I will attempt to show what some of our wisest people have always held is the real importance of the United States of America; those principles which, if understood and put in practice, will fan a flame that can shine forth anew to illuminate and advance the destiny of the entire human race.

The basic theory here is that we are in the early stages of our fourth quantum evolutionary shift on this planet, from what is called the Fourth Kingdom to the Fifth. We have had three such shifts already; from the mineral kingdom to the vegetable kingdom, from the vegetable to the animal kingdom, and from the animal to the human kingdom. The three previous shifts have been involuntary; rocks had no say in becoming vegetable, vegetables had no say in becoming animal, and so on. But one of the essential aspects of the new state of being into which we are already beginning to enter is that it can only be successfully brought about through the understanding and choice of the individual creature that is the human being. That choice can only be made when the individual actually sees for him/herself the truth of the matter, and that seeing can only happen when the individual is truly free to use his/her God-given bodily senses, mind, and heart in the way they were intended to be used, free from any undue influence whether positive or negative. This freedom of the individual is the very heart of the American Experiment, and it is now time for us to awaken to its real nature and its real potential. We must now allow our hearts to awaken and to open us to spiritual realities. The purpose of this presentation is primarily to comment on these matters, but first let us face facts about our current state of affairs and how necessary it has become that we bring about rapid and fundamental change.

I was born in 1938. At that time the world was just beginning to become aware of the storm that was gathering in the form of World War II. There was still a widespread if mostly subconscious feeling that World War I had taught us that we must never do such a thing again; that our leaders would insist that we find better ways to settle our differences. World War I was "the war to end all wars".

At that time we were still largely an agricultural nation and while we were well on the way to becoming an almost exclusively industrial society, the war greatly boosted the speed of that change as factories churned out the vast array of products associated with the war effort and our industrial capacity expanded accordingly. The "military-industrial complex" entered its heyday; its influence on our government and our media set us on a path that has brought us to the point where our military expenditures now total nearly half of our total national budget. Other large corporate entities have not been slow to take full advantage of these dynamics, expanding their influence in our elective and legislative processes together with consolidating ownership of (and thus controlling) nearly all our media. The result of all this has been the near ruin of our democracy.

For one who was young in the post WWII days when our economy was booming, there was "a Ford in your future", and having emerged victorious in the war we felt that we were on a path to becoming a "shining city on a hill", spreading democracy, peace, and goodwill across the globe, it is simply heartbreaking to realize how different a course we have actually taken. At that time our present situation would have been scarcely imaginable.

The American Experiment is teetering on the brink of failure. Far from having shown the world the results of a national insistence on ensuring that the individual human is valued, understood, educated, and encouraged to grow in the most important ways, we seem instead to be intent on demonstrating what happens when the richest nation in the world runs the course of self-centered materialism to its ultimate outcome. We have almost completely failed to realize that freedom cannot be separated from responsibility, when it becomes simply license. We accept as normal, even as inevitable, such a stew of ignorance, corruption, and selfish shortsightedness in our social, economic, and political affairs that we have allowed our precious democracy to all but disappear, it having now been almost completely taken over by large corporate entities so viciously ignorant in their behavior that they have almost ruined our economy, dulled our society into a stupor of consumerism (paradoxically combined with an absolutely frantic pace of life), and so trashed our environment that there is serious question as to whether or not we may have irreparably breached the narrow spectrum of natural conditions within which life as we know it can exist. Let us examine several of our most serious crises, bearing in mind at all times that we the people have allowed all this to happen, having failed terribly in our responsibilities as citizens of a democratic society, where the buck stops at the individual citizen.

In this effort I will barely scratch the surface of the troubles that now exist; my purpose is not to wade through the virtually bottomless swamp of our errors, important examples of which can be found practically anywhere one chooses to look. But it is necessary to examine enough of those mistakes to make it unequivocally clear that we have one central problem that is responsible for virtually all the others, and that it is futile to think we can deal effectively with these individual crises until we solve our fundamental root problem; the near destruction of our democracy by a corporate oligarchy.

POPULATION

Throughout the following discussion we should keep in mind a central factor that has greatly increased each of the troubles we will consider; the exponentially-increasing number of human beings who continue to take up life on this planet. The "population bomb" has gone off; it took three or four million years for the human population to reach two billion. And how long to reach three billion? Thirty years. It currently stands at over seven billion and we can, if things go on as they continue to do, expect to reach ten billion by 2050. Surely it is not hard to see that this constant increase in numbers puts enormous pressure on all the systems that support human life. The sheer numbers of meals, houses, jobs, clothes, etc, etc, etc. that are now required every day dwarfs the numbers that applied even one generation before my own. There were only sixty million people in the United States when my parents were young; now we have three hundred and thirteen million. So it is virtually useless to address any single crisis without taking into account the effect of the population explosion on that issue. A planet with finite resources cannot indefinitely sustain an increasing population. We must face this crisis (virtually the only one that is not directly due to the activities of the corporate oligarchy) squarely and effectively if we expect to really fix almost anything else; one of the first things we can and should do is a study of the carrying capacity of our planet to establish how many people it can support at various levels of income; then we can make policy on the basis of fact rather than fantasy.

THE ENVIRONMENT

Since the beginning of the Industrial Revolution, when machines began to perform the vast bulk of physical activities in which our industries engage, we have poured a steady stream of carbon dioxide into our atmosphere, because CO_2 is the major byproduct of our energy production system, especially since we started using coal and then oil as our chief energy sources. The most damaging result of this massive amount of CO_2, so far beyond what would naturally occur, has been what we call "global warming". (The term "climate change" appears to be taking the place of "global warming", since we have been experiencing extraordinary cold as well as extraordinary heat [both were predicted], but the overall trend is undeniably one of warming.) There is a natural cycle of which we have been aware for a long time, part of which includes periods of warming but there is no longer any doubt among sincere observers that the enormous amount of CO_2 (together with other gases such as methane) that we have poured into our atmosphere has greatly and dangerously altered the natural rhythm of the present cycle.

One of the most severe effects of this exaggeration of the natural cycle is the melting of our polar ice caps, which is proceeding at a truly alarming (and increasing) rate, leading to a rise in sea level that is not just noticeable but which even at this early stage is beginning to overwhelm low-lying nations such as the Maldives. Heads are spinning with calculations and minds are reeling at the foreseeable effects of the now-unavoidable increase in these conditions (even if we put the pedal to the metal in reverse, it's too late to avoid a severe increase in effects; this car takes time to stop); just look at a map of human settlements in the U.S.A. alone (e.g. New York, New Jersey, Norfolk, Miami, New Orleans, Los Angeles, San Francisco, Seattle) that are close enough to sea level to be threatened in the foreseeable future. And we should realize that it's not just the ice caps that are melting; so are the Himalayan glaciers, which supply fresh water for something like two billion people. And Glacier National Park is expected to have <u>no</u> glaciers by 2035. How bright do the red lights have to get before we notice them flashing?

Of equal concern are the effects that this human-exaggerated climate change can be expected to produce on the weather. These range from extreme heat-related events in some areas to extreme cold-related events in others; we are already seeing extreme winters and extreme summers as well; floods, droughts, fires, and

11

extraordinarily severe storms (all of which have been predicted by those who have been seriously studying the situation). Is it really so surprising that we get in trouble when we tinker with the natural heat/cold systems of our planet to the point where our major cold-storage centers (the arctic and antarctic ice caps) are disappearing? To so casually wreck the natural balance between heat and cold on our planet is to ignore the fact that God set these things up in stunningly precise balance. And for those life forms such as ourselves that can only exist within a relatively narrow band of natural conditions, a very delicate balance as well. We would do well to realize that God is not mocked; nature bats last.

Is it so difficult to see that the source of this CO_2 is industry (together with the products it produces)? Or that industry has always been far more concerned with the money it generates than with its effects on the environment or anything else other than profits? Admittedly, these negative effects have crept up on us; it took a far-sighted person indeed to predict these things at the beginning of the Industrial Revolution (some folks did, though), but in recent decades these effects have become obvious to anyone who was paying attention. A great many people are waking up to the seriousness of this situation but we have not yet reached the critical mass that will be necessary to turn things around. And we must not overlook the fact that the energy industry continues to oppose regulatory reform with every means at their disposal (like virtually if not literally every other industry whose activities have harmful effects), smoothly assuring an amazingly unquestioning public that everything is just fine. Shame on them, shame on us.

While we're talking about energy we must not pass by one of the most alarming aspects of our addiction to massive energy use; nukes. One has to be blind indeed not to recognize what an astonishing achievement splitting the atom was, or the potential uses for the enormous energy that is produced by nuclear reactors. But it is unwise to let our desire for things like electric popcorn poppers blind us to the problems inherent in this method of producing electricity.

These problems are significant and as yet insurmountable. Among the worst of them is the fact that the byproducts of nuclear fission are dangerous and will remain so for tens of thousands of years. What will this mean for our children's children, should there still be a habitable planet for them to live on? We tinker around with fantasies like burying nuclear waste in salt deposits or encasing them in glass, but does anyone seriously think that these methods will be viable for tens of thousands of years? And what about, for just one example, that underground waste at Hanford, Washington that has been creeping for decades toward the Columbia River? This is just the tip of the nuclear iceberg, but we don't seem to notice or care about such things. Things like the numerous deaths of uranium miners, or the fact that human error, computer error, and natural disasters are unavoidable; each of them is not a question of if, but when. We have already seen Chernobyl, Three Mile Island, and now possibly the worst of all, Fukushima, where as I write three reactors have melted down. It will take perhaps twenty years to make them safe, if that can be done. A hundred thousand people have been forced from their homes, with no idea when or if they can ever go back. At the height of the crisis, the possibility of a "worst case scenario" had the Japanese government considering the evacuation of Tokyo. Neither the government or the nuclear industry in Japan (or here) appear to be telling the truth about the seriousness of the current or future state of affairs (for example, they claim to have these plants in a stable condition, but today's news reported that levels of radiation have risen to the point where even their robots are unusable).

What is it going to take to make us wake up to the facts of the case here? What if there is another serious earthquake in Japan, or here (where several of our nukes are also on or near earthquake faults)? Even if we accept the highly questionable idea that the effects of nuclear radiation are only significant in large doses, we should realize that massive doses can and do and will occur whenever we have a significant accident at a nuclear plant. People will be hurt; a substantial area around Chernobyl is uninhabitable and will remain so for a very long time. We can expect the same thing with Fukushima. One very experienced nuclear scientist has predicted that over time we can expect a million cases of cancer from this disaster (some kinds of radiation can take a very long time for their damage to manifest). Is this really necessary? Can we not yet realize that behind the smooth assurances of those who want to build nukes is primarily a desire to make money, not concern for the welfare of the public or the planet?

How about nuclear war? "It won't be water but fire next time", says the Bible. Virtually every nation with the capacity to do so seems to be trying to join the "nuclear club"; to possess the Big Bargaining Chip. We scream bloody murder about Iran trying to do so (not so loud about North Korea, India, Pakistan or any of the other members of the nuclear club because they already have nukes; they're club members) but our protestation lacks a certain force in the eyes of the world because we have more nukes than anybody, and we insist that that's perfectly OK. We alone have enough nukes to destroy human civilization (and God knows how much else along with it). This is intelligent? This is sane? This is loving? Oops, excuse that last one; I got carried away.

But when you think about it, what good could a nuke really do for any small nation when the Big Dogs have such vastly superior power? Does anyone really think

Iran would drop a nuke on Israel or the U.S.? Their entire nation would be reduced to rubble in hours, and they know it. It's the Big Bargaining Chip that's so attractive, because so long as the international community plays the fear-based power game instead of the love-based cooperative game, the biggest gun gets to sit at the head of the table. This is how animal affairs have always worked. Now this basic behavior must change; we'll expand on that later. For the moment, we should realize that nuclear fission is a total non-starter; with <u>far</u> more to be lost than to be gained through its use. And when will we begin to question the necessity of using every conceivable electrical gadget that is foisted on us by people whose primary concern is to make money? Why can't we see not just the possible significance, but the growing necessity of consuming less? Can we not see that at the very heart of the nuclear problem are the corporations that profit from the nuclear enterprise? These are the people who assured us in the beginning that nuclear power would be "too cheap to meter", safe as mothers' milk (which now contains numerous poisonous substances because of the pollution of our air, water, and food), and most recently, "environmentally friendly". How can it be that we keep on taking their word for <u>anything</u>? Where is the scrutiny that should be constantly applied to such dangerous endeavors? It is the height of naivete to believe that the Nuclear Regulatory Commission will protect us, any more than the Environmental Protection

Agency will, because the nuclear industry controls the government agencies that are supposed to protect the public from the dangers posed by that industry. In which connection we should note that so dangerous are its operations, the nuclear industry can't get insurance on them, so the government provides it. We'll examine how such a thing could happen more closely when we get to politics.

We should not lose sight of the fact that we are running out of oil (which, of course, provides a first-rate excuse for the coalies and nukesters to hustle their product). Sure, there is still a fair amount of it left but it's becoming steadily more difficult, expensive, and environmentally dangerous to get at. We've used up the world's oil supply so freely that we are at or near "peak oil", or the point at which foreseeable use exceeds foreseeable supply. And, by the way, we are supposedly in such desperate need of oil that we currently pay over four dollars a gallon for gas; but we still export enormous amounts of oil. Certainly not from humanitarianism but because there's money to be made. Forget coal; it's a filthy way to make electricity. From the mine through the power generation process to the disposal of waste, coal has significant harmful environmental effects, including release of mercury, sulfur dioxide, nitrogen oxides and particulates into the atmosphere. Coal-fired power plants also happen to be our biggest source of CO_2; even greater than automobiles, trucks, planes, or trains. And yet again, the reason coal continues to be a problem is because the corporations that profit from it continue to care only about the money they make, and they continue to mislead us into thinking that it's OK; not to worry. We swallow it hook, line, and sinker because we're addicted to using ever increasing amounts of energy for whatever device can be invented to feed our habit; we want to believe that it's all right to keep on this way, so we accept the blandishments of industry and refuse to pay attention to the reality of the situation.

We could expand this list indefinitely. The simple truth is, our air is filled with harmful substances which are the byproducts of industries whose operators do not care at all about the harmful effects of their activities; they are primarily interested in money. Our water is also terribly polluted, and for the exact same reason; industry spews a stunning cocktail of harmful substances into our water supply, heedless of the harm it causes. One of the latest horrors is "fracking"; a cutting-edge technique for extracting oil and natural gas by fracturing underground rock formations in which they are stored. They pump enormous amounts of mephistophelian substances into our groundwater with the result that in several places people cannot drink their water; in fact, they can light it with a match! Again, it is large corporate entities that do these things, lying to us repeatedly about the damage they do, and we go along with it because we like the things we can do with the energy that these corporations produce and we don't much care about the damage they do until it comes right to our door. The corporations know that; they count on our unwillingness and/or inability to think seriously about the harm they're causing, and it works very well indeed. For them, that is; not so well for the environment or for ourselves a little further down the road than we're willing to look. No heroin addict was ever a greater sucker for his dealer than we are for these corporados who take such advantage of our unwillingness to think. Our environment has been terribly damaged and the damage continues to worsen; we must wake up and deal with this reality, and soon.

AGRICULTURE

Another area in which we have turned over vitally important functions to enormous corporations is our food supply, distribution, and sale. There was a time when our food was produced primarily by small family farmers, and it was done organically because the agricultural chemicals with which we now bombard our land, air, water, fieldworkers, and farmside communities didn't exist. We hadn't yet learned to recoil in horror if there was a blemish on our apple or our bread was any color but lily white (a wonderful example of this attitude is the prevalence of "white bread"; we pay to have natural vitamins removed, and then pay more to have artificial ones put in), and we were far better nourished than we are now, when our food supply is contaminated with an astonishing brew of chemicals that are well known to cause illnesses ranging from food poisoning to cancer. Not to mention "genetic engineering", in which man blindly plays God yet again; fifty countries have now banned or restricted genetically modified organisms but we don't even require that they be identified on the food that contains them. And watching the evening news, one has to wonder if our brains have been getting anything like their proper nourishment, particularly in the case of our children, in whom the early years are critical for brain development. Seriously. How else can we explain the near total absence of the ability to think deeply about anything important? Late flash: today's news reports that a new study suggests that part of the large recent increase in autism in children is due to the prevalence of high-fructose corn syrup, which inhibits the presence of zinc, which is important in the formation of young brains.

Basically, what happened was that we needed to protect our troops in World War Two from malaria in foreign lands and we discovered that DDT did the job nicely, killing the mosquitos that carried malaria. After the war the Department of Agriculture pointed out to America's farmers (greatly encouraged by the industries that were gearing up to manufacture agricultural chemicals) that they could use it to control common pests in their fields. Then new pesticides (kill the bugs!) and herbicides (kill the weeds!) were produced and pushed on farmers at an accelerating rate. Early on, alarmed observers such as the wonderful Rachel Carson ("Silent Spring") realized that these chemicals were migrating off the farm in a variety of ways and causing very significant harm to the environment, such as weakening the shells of birds' eggs so that they couldn't hatch, or killing off "good" (and ecologically important) bugs along with the "bad" ones. But by that time large corporate farms had developed, and they exerted enormous influence on Congress to approve whatever they wanted them to. So this way of farming, using unnatural fertilizers and chemicals to kill bugs and weeds became the norm. Small farmers generally felt obliged to follow these same practices in order to compete with the big guys, but they began to fall by the wayside because of the lower prices that agribusiness could charge because of the "economy of scale", whereby large outfits could buy supplies cheaper than small ones because they bought much larger amounts and they could charge lower prices because their sales were so much larger. So the family farm faded into the background and huge agricultural corporations burgeoned. As did the chemical companies. So we are left with inferior food and a damaged environment.

For several decades people have been awakening to these realities and demanding real ("organic") food, but its higher price and the ongoing willingness of the general public to accept the blandishments of agribusiness have made it difficult for the movement to really take hold. Still, people continue to awaken and organic food sales continue to grow. But yet again, large corporate entities control this vital aspect of our lives, and they do so with an eye far more to profit for themselves than to the health of the human beings they supposedly serve. And they get away with it because we let them make the rules. As one of our major corporate criminals said, "You know the Golden Rule; he who has the gold rules."

FORESTRY

One subject that has caught the attention of many people, especially since the remarkable John Muir bestrode the mountains and valleys of the Sierra Nevada, is what we've allowed to be done to our nation's forests. In spite of the fact that we in the U.S.A. have preserved quite a number of wild places by global standards, the fact remains that we have cut down virtually all of this nation's extraordinary original endowment of forests. When we white folks got here and began the process of taking the land away from the people who lived on it when we arrived (who loved and protected the land, which they recognized as their Mother), the continental United States was, with the exception of the Great Plains and the deserts, covered with forests so large and so beautiful that we can hardly imagine it today. But those forests consisted of an obviously valuable commodity; timber. So we set about destroying them as fast as the timber industry could contrive to do. Those original forests never come back; a different kind of forest grows in their place, and it can take hundreds, even thousands of years to do so. Compared to its original state, our country now resembles the head of a cancer patient, with tufts of hair here and there instead of the full, luxuriant growth that previously covered it. Ninety-five percent of our giant redwood forests have been cut; a fact that simply breaks the heart of anyone who has ever felt the reality of a giant redwood tree in a virgin old-growth forest (commonly referred to as "cathedral forests"), and this holds true for all the other forest types that originally graced this land.

Of course we have had a legitimate need for timber. Of course it was appropriate to use this natural resource to build things with. Of course it was appropriate for the people who did the work of converting trees to lumber to be compensated for their work. But where is the balance? Where is the realization of the many other very significant values in a natural forest besides that of timber? What we have seen here is the same old story; those who made money from this activity didn't (and don't) want to hear about "balance" or anything else that prevents them from raking in as much money as they can possibly manage to get. So our forests have disappeared into the pockets of, yet again, the corporados. "White man clever, but not wise." (Chief Seattle)

HEALTH CARE

We must face some facts about our health care system. Nearly all developed nations have some form of single-payer health system, in which the government is basically the insurer for everyone. This is classic insurance, in which everyone pays a relatively small amount into the kitty and those who need it take out a relatively large amount compared to what they put in. It works because most people don't need expensive operations or other costly care, so they carry those who do. And in a society of real human beings the former group doesn't begrudge the latter, even if only because they know that but for the grace of God they'd be in the latter group too.

Evidently the United States is severely lacking in humanity because we are one of the few "developed" nations who allow health care for profit; that is, for it to be provided by corporate entities who so arrange things (as we shall see in the section on politics) that they can make enormous amounts of money by providing the services of doctors, hospitals, drugs, nursing homes; all the things people so desperately need when they get sick, injured, or old. The profits of the health insurance industry and the pharmaceutical industry make up a very substantial part of our total expenditures for health care, and these industries provide far less care for far more money than almost all other developed nations. This situation is a national disgrace; so many people suffer and die needlessly because they simply cannot afford the care they need, but the industry keeps right on telling us that we have the best system in the world, that other nations' single-payer systems don't work (simply untrue), and that any system but the one that benefits the corporados so much is "socialism" (which is a terrible thing of course, because... well, just because). And so many of us continue to believe this garbage.

Recently the U.S. altered its health care system with a plan that was put forward by President Obama. This plan has been viciously attacked by so-called conservatives (who know next to nothing about the meaning of conservatism, which comes from the same root as "conservation"), who insist that it's "socialism"; that it picks their pockets to pay for the well-deserved troubles of their lazy neighbors who can't be bothered to "pull themselves up by their bootstraps", and so on. These notions are so ill-informed and heartless that they're unworthy of discussion, but the plan has also been criticized by those of a more liberal persuasion, on radically different grounds that boil down to the simple fact that the plan doesn't go nearly far enough in seeing to it that every brother and sister who needs medical care can and will get it.

When the idea of health care reform came up during President Obama's first term it was immediately fought tooth and nail by those who engage in health care for profit. It is worth remembering that this matter already came up fairly recently, in the Clinton administration when the President of the United States announced that our health care system was broken and that he (with the First Lady in charge) intended to fix it. It took about three months for the subject to be reduced to ashes; we just didn't hear about it any more. Why? For the same reason that Obama's plan was reduced to relatively minor changes; the insurance and drug industries had the power to defeat any really meaningful reform.

The way they did this was exquisitely laid out on television by a remarkable person who had served for many years in a top position in one of the largest health insurance companies in the country. It's quite a story; he quit his job when he happened to go to a "health fair" at the county fairgrounds somewhere in the South. He saw the horse stalls at the fairgrounds converted into sheeted tables and booths in which people who couldn't afford health care could get some relief. As he looked at the long lines of suffering people he had an epiphany; he realized that those numbers he'd crunched all those years, trying to ensure that the bottom line (keep the stockholders happy) was maximized, actually represented suffering human beings, not just ciphers in an insurance company office. The host of the television program was astonished; he said "You mean to tell me that all those years you had those numbers in front of you; you knew who was under-insured and who was uninsured, yet your heart was so hardened that you didn't allow yourself to realize that these were people?!" To which the executive replied "YES! That's exactly what I'm trying to tell you! This is how it works, and not just in the insurance industry, you can be sure." He then proceeded to predict what the insurance and drug industries would do to defeat meaningful reform, and that was precisely what happened. Seventy percent of the public sanely and morally wanted a single-payer system like almost everyone else in the civilized world but that wasn't even "on the table", which is simply astonishing. Isn't this supposed to be a democracy? Do the wishes of seventy percent of the citizenry count for nothing? Really. Think about it. Then the weak alternative of some kind of "public option" (which would also, although to a much lesser extent, have limited the power of the health-care-for-profit industry) was completely shot down, and we got a patchwork of measures which, while they did improve certain aspects of the situation, were far from what was needed or what was demanded by the American people. So here we go again; the corporados are perfectly willing to let their brothers and sisters suffer and die, so long as the industry's profits are maximized. And they're still trying to dismantle even the weak Obama plan. This is a shameful situation; it is not going to play well at the Pearly Gates.

EDUCATION

As we have observed, most of us have no interest in the real higher education of life, which is a pity because these matters concern each and every one of us. They affect us every minute of our lives on earth and they will continue to affect us thereafter; how much better use we would make of this life if we understood its real nature and purpose, especially in view of the major changes that are in our immediate future. (By the way, just in case anyone should ask, the purpose of life is totally simple and easy to understand; the purpose of life is to understand the purpose of life. Seriously. More or less...)

In terms of our ability to deal with what lies immediately ahead of us our lack of understanding of 1) what we are, 2) where we come from, 3) where we're going, and 4) what's going on, is crippling. Every educational institution in this nation should have courses in Principles of Living, in which now-common human knowledge (such as the fact that matter is not solid, that space is infinite, or the great realities which our religions and mystics have put before us) is brought to bear on each of these four great questions. Obviously that is not something that most boards of education would consider seriously at this time, but I predict that coming events will radically alter that attitude.

What, then, do our educational institutions teach our young people? Scarcely, it would seem, how (or why) to read, write, or speak more than a fraction of their native language. The quality of education in the United States today ranks shockingly low among developed nations. Far from turning out trained minds skilled in the exercise of our God-given intellect and fired with enthusiasm for ongoing learning about important matters, our educational institutions are failing even to teach students the material skills that our technological society now requires; many other nations are doing a far better job in this regard, and their students are consequently ahead of ours in the globalized employment line. Let a few statistics speak for themselves: a recent poll showed that forty-two percent of American adults are unaware that the U.S. declared its independence in 1776; of those under age thirty, sixty-nine percent. Twenty-five percent of Americans don't know which country we broke away from. Seventy-three percent of Americans don't know why we engaged in the Cold War. Forty-four percent of us don't know what the Bill of Rights is (a good indication of why we placidly accept such dangerous, un-American horrors as the Patriot Act, the National

Defense Authorization Act, or the Foreign Intelligence Surveillance Act). Two out of three Americans can't name the three branches of our government or name a single Supreme Court justice. And a recent poll of the Oklahoma public school system showed that seventy-seven percent of the students didn't know who George Washington was. For that matter, twenty or thirty years back, out of fifty people in a pool of prospective jurors in one of our Southern states, not a single one knew who Adolph Hitler was. And a Gallup Poll just revealed that forty-six percent of Americans believe that the human being was created in its present form (presumably instantly) within the last ten thousand years. God help us.

Under such conditions it is hard to see how anyone could think of us as an educated nation, but this concerns our legislators so little that currently our schools are lacking such obvious necessities as pencils and paper, or (as in our local schools in Northern California) even the busing to get the kids to school at all. This while school boards in some places furiously debate such radiantly intelligent matters as how to counter the teaching of evolution. As our economy continues to weaken because of the corporate depredations we have been discussing, funds are being cut by government at all levels; not from the massive handouts given to large corporations, of course, but from vital services to ordinary human beings, such as education. In the case of busing, our kids up here got together and descended on Sacramento with the result that the buses will continue to run, at least for a while. We had better follow the students' example; we should think seriously about how vital education is to everything our children will be doing in the future, and we should do whatever it takes to bestir our elected representatives to also think seriously about it. We must face the fact that the reason why massive corporate welfare continues while real human need is given short shrift to the point where large numbers of people suffer and even die is because the corporatocracy controls our government. This has become the central fact of our national existence; wouldn't you think that our schools would be educating our children about it?

THE ECONOMY

In days of old our goods were produced by craftsmen working either alone or in small groups, using what we now call "hand tools". Then along came the Industrial Revolution. Along with steam, water wheels used the power of rivers to turn shafts that powered a variety of machinery, and that machinery was operated by increasingly large numbers of people whose skills were no longer necessarily those of the craftsman; just about anyone could handle most demands of factory labor. And the craftsman began to disappear, since he could hardly compete with mass production from factories. Then we figured out how to generate electricity, which allowed us to use electric motors to turn our shafts almost anywhere and which led to enormous industrial growth as factories were built to manufacture all sorts of products in far greater quantities than had ever been available before. Then we prioritized coal, which took over as our major energy source (it's still the top source of electricity generation worldwide). And then we developed oil, which currently provides about forty percent of our total energy production in the U.S.A.

The oil industry is foremost in our thoughts, since it fuels our automobiles. Which means that they have us where any corporado dreams of having us, right by the gas tank. They can charge us whatever they want to, up to the point where we simply cannot afford to pay. So Exxon, for example, makes so much money that the zeros extend out to where only the Hubble telescope can see them. BP gets to trash our southern coastal waters and onshore ecosystems and basically walks away from it with minimal reparations and almost zero prosecution for their terribly harmful negligence (while they cajole us with silken TV ads that assure us that everything's really nice down there now. It isn't). And the industry continues to slither away with an enormous amount of government welfare, including about four billion dollars of tax breaks each year. They certainly don't call it "welfare" though, any more than they call it "entitlements", although they certainly feel entitled to it. No; those now-negative terms are reserved for poor people in real need of real help.

We now pay roughly four dollars a gallon for gas, and a substantial part of that is due to speculators, who bid the price up in anticipation of what they can be sure will be future price increases for crude oil. The average person has nothing to say in the matter, except in the event that he can persuade his elected representatives to do something about it. This is less than likely, since almost all of our elected representatives are accustomed to doing the will of the oil companies far more than that of their constituents. Along with the will of the other large corporate entities that now control the United States of America. Actually, high prices for gas are an excellent thing, in view of the effects that our automobile exhausts have on the environment. We simply must convert to clean, renewable energy. And that inescapably means that at least in the short run we will have to learn to get along with less, as humanity has always done until relatively recently and most of which still does, with the exception of the "developed countries" such as ourselves. With five percent of the world's population we use about a quarter of its energy; how can we continue to pretend that this is right? Or that it doesn't matter if it's wrong?

It seems clear that even if we put in place every method of alternative energy generation that we currently possess; wind, water, geothermal, solar, etc., we couldn't come near generating the amount of energy we currently use. We will simply have to accept a lower level of energy use, at least until we can properly (renewably) generate the greater amount. And we may be able to do so; who knows what new technologies will come into being if we just get busy supporting their development? But there is no longer any excuse for failing to bite the bullet and embark on a crash course in that development. Won't it be worth the sacrifice if it allows us to have a still-beautiful planet to live on or indeed, to still be able to live here at all?

We spend a very substantial part of our income on oil and natural gas for our cars and our home heating, and as usual we're almost completely at the mercy of the corporate entities that provide that energy, caring for almost nothing but maximizing their profits. They will convert to sustainable energy if and when they see that it will be sufficiently profitable, but they'll wait to do so until they've sold every possible drop of fossil fuels. They are not just unconcerned with what they're doing to the environment; they deliberately (and with terrible success) fight against environmental protection because they see it as limiting the amount of money they can make. And consider this; they now have available, and of course plan to develop, five times more oil and gas than experts say our environment can stand without catastrophic consequences.

What about our personal financial realities? Almost all of us use banks to store whatever income we can generate beyond our immediate cash needs. We also use investment and, to a lesser degree, higher risk speculation to store and hopefully increase our assets through stocks and bonds (We do this not just individually but in group investments such as our IRAs, pension funds, etc.). So long as the banks behave responsibly and the companies in which we invest prosper, this system works quite well, as it did so spectacularly from right after World War II until 2007-8, when it became obvious that something had gone terribly wrong. Well, what went wrong?

When President Eisenhower left office in 1961 he issued a message which will stand as one of history's most significant unheeded warnings; he told us to be strongly on guard against the influence of what he called the "military-industrial complex". He knew whereof he spoke; as commander of the winning team in World War II and then President, he was well aware of the activities of the defense industry; of the multiplicity of large contractors and smaller subcontractors who had profited so greatly from the war effort and who, of course, had churned out the material which made it possible to win the war. The benefits of industry are certainly real and generally recognized, but it is the <u>dangers</u> in the activities of large corporate entities operating in an environment virtually free of morality or regulation, that are to be feared and guarded against. This last is what Eisenhower was specifically warning us about; allowing these large corporations to operate without close, effective regulation. What regulation there was, turned out to be astonishingly ineffective in terms of reining in the corporate abuse of our environment, our health, our economy, and our society, primarily through dynamics which we will explore in the section on politics.

The emergence of the trans-national corporation signaled the beginning of the end of nearly every vital system under which this nation had previously operated. It pushed us into an era of "globalism" which on the face of it, as corporate propaganda constantly assured us, seemed to mean arm-in-arm brotherly and sisterly cooperation with our fellow human beings around the globe, nothing less and nothing more (well, the sisters were basically left out until the sixties slowly began to change things; both sexism and racism are still deeply ingrained in our society). But it meant nothing of the kind in reality; what it really turned out to mean was accelerated stripping away of the resources of other, weaker nations for our own profit and enjoyment, with negligible benefit together with great harm to the people in those nations (except for the compliant politicians and generals that enabled it all and got rich from so doing). Then, in an enormously important development, our jobs began to disappear as the corporations built factories in third world countries where labor was dirt cheap compared to what they had been used to paying here at home. They didn't have to do this; they were making plenty of money but they wanted more; a whole lot more. There was some blue-collar grumbling but not a great deal, since things were still humming along at a fair clip and jobs could still be found for most of the people displaced by the emigration of factory jobs. Another reason that complaints were weak was the fact that the power of labor unions had been steadily declining since the sixties, due largely to the growing control large corporations had over Congress, which began to undo decades of effort on behalf of ordinary workers in favor of legislation that helped the rich people who, after all, got members of Congress elected and whose lobbyists were constantly close at hand to tell them what to do. Here's a pertinent quote from my own experience, uttered by a top member of our county Planning Department: "I don't give a good goddamn what (anyone) thinks; I just want someone to tell me what to do so I don't have to think." Candid, certainly, but much too common an attitude on the part of our public servants.

Then, in the Reagan era, a whole new phenomenon began to appear. In keeping with the "neo-conservative" view of things in which corporations (large ones, not your little one) should be as unrestricted as possible so that they could make oceans of money, which would supposedly "trickle down" to the common folk in the form of jobs, Reagan oversaw a large scale program of deregulation, through which the foxes were given charge of the financial, environmental, and political henhouses, and they immediately set about gorging on hens.

Among the worst effects of this deregulation was the freedom that was given to the financial industry to invent new ways of using (your) money to make (them) money. A whole madhouse full of new financial instruments designed to make money in the most questionable ways came into being, and almost nobody seemed to notice that this was extremely dangerous. It was bound to blow up eventually because it was not built on anything real, but only on sleight-of-hand, smokescreens, and alchemical technical definitions that no so-called regulator seemed willing or able to decipher (a few did but they were not listened to because so much money was being made).

The most significant examples of this madness were a class of financial instruments called "derivatives"; a loose term for what were essentially insurance policies on investments that involved risk; a bet, so to speak, on the degree of likelihood of the failure of a given investment. It had been common for many years for derivatives of a sort to be used to hedge against future fluctuations in value in commodity markets such as agriculture, metals, or currencies; now they were put to very different uses.

A group of whiz kids at J.P.Morgan were whooping it up one weekend when they came up with a brilliant idea. They were brainstorming ways to reduce the risk that was necessarily a part of their loans (specifically a large loan to Exxon to enable them to clean up the Exxon-Valdez spill), and the idea arose that that risk could be separated from the asset itself and sold to a party who agreed to act as insurer. You wouldn't call it insurance, because insurance was restricted to a degree by various regulations and you certainly wanted to avoid that, so they decided to call these insurance policies "credit default swaps"; a splendid term that very few people outside the industry would understand but which most folks (like the manager of your pension fund) would assume was just fine because it sounded good and it came, after all, from the "experts". A fee would be paid, of course, and the risk (for Morgan) would be eliminated, as (through later arrangements) would the sizable amount of money that normally was required to be set aside to guarantee payment on investments that went bad. Hey presto! They found a willing insurer and off they went, into a new and unregulated ("dark") market that was about to grow like a malignant cancer.

With the risk and locked-up capital of the Exxon loan so tidily dealt with, Morgan not surprisingly decided to deal similarly with more of their loans; three hundred of them. It didn't take long for the other large financial institutions to catch on to the possibilities here; they jumped on board and stoked the engines, swapping risk and freeing up funds for further fun and games. And along came a magnificent opportunity in the form of collateralized mortgage obligations (CMOs), which took advantage of the booming real estate market by selling mortgages to anyone who could fog a mirror and turning the holding of said mortgages into a no-risk proposition for the issuer of the mortgage by selling them, bundled together with others of varying degrees of risk, as investments in themselves. This radically drove up the real estate market, which took off like a rocket (as did the other debt swaps; so much money was being made) because just about anyone could get a mortgage. Never mind the fate that the lenders knew awaited the poor "sub-prime" mortgage holder.

Another important wrinkle was added with the "naked" credit swap, in which a credit default swap (insurance policy) was sold not just to the owner of a given financial instrument but to anyone else who wanted to buy a policy on that particular instrument. This basically turned the whole thing into a casino, with investors madly betting on the bets that bet on the bets. This is a great simplification of what went on; the whole mad scene was complicated enough to challenge a PhD in economics, but this is the gist of it. The whole thing was doomed to blow up sooner or later because 1) it was basically a pyramid scheme, built not on sound investments but on bets "derived" from those investments (far too many of which, e.g. all those sub-prime mortgages, weren't sound at all) and 2) since it was a "dark" market, almost wholly unregulated, only a fraction of the money necessary to pay off all these bets if they went wrong (as they were bound to eventually) had been set aside. When the whole house of cards collapsed there were sixty-two trillion dollars worth of these obligations outstanding and only about six trillion available to pay them off. So these great, respectable, important financial institutions started to crumble, and we all know what happened next. Our government put them back on their feet, with trillions of dollars taken from the pockets of their victims, the American people. We got the whole load of bullshoot about how these financial giants were "too big to fail", and how the entire economy would just collapse if we didn't immediately pour (more) trillions of dollars into their pockets. We (our elected representatives) bought it hook, line, and sinker. To date we've given or lent these howling malefactors, in one form or another, twenty-nine trillion dollars. Incredibly, these giants are now bigger than ever. They have more money than before, and they continue to pay their top executives absolutely obscene amounts of money. But are they pouring out loans to small businesses that need them? Are they going full tilt to rescue their victims who lost or are in danger of losing their homes? Nothing of the sort. They're stuffing themselves even more than they were before, with no regard for the wreckage they caused. Almost none of them have faced any kind of legal consequences of their awful deeds. And we stand for it.

We should also note the shocking performance of our governmental regulatory agencies in this matter, as the derivative schemes started to really take off. Basically, they did nothing. There was some concern expressed, but the "free market" philosophy prevailed; quite easily, since nobody seemed to be able to establish which agency or agencies (e.g. the Commodity Futures Trading Commission, the Treasury Department, the Securities and Exchange Commission, the Federal Reserve Board) had jurisdiction over this new market. The new chair of the CFTC saw clearly that something highly dangerous was brewing and tried her best to generate meaningful action, but she didn't stand a chance. Nobody wanted to hamper the growth of this so-profitable new market. And then Congress (under the influence of the financial industry, of course) passed legislation that effectively prevented federal regulation in this area. So much for the effectiveness of governmental watchdog agencies.

How about the executive branch and Congress? We have already seen how Congress viewed the whole thing; hands off. When things hit the fan, the people in the administration responsible for dealing with the situation had no idea what to do (in spite of the fact that they were "experts"; the President drew them from the very industry that was crumbling). When the first big firm (Bear Stearns) failed, they decided that since Bear owed so much to so many they were too big to fail, so the government bailed them out. But when the next one (Lehman) went down, they decided to let it go, because they didn't feel it appropriate to send the message that they'd bail out one and all. So Lehman went bankrupt and the rest of the industry shuddered (and sprang into action), because they knew what was coming and if the government dealt with them the way they had with Lehman they were out of luck. Not to worry; the ultimate decision by the government (surprise!) was that they were too big to fail, so they (we) bailed them out.

I think the whole concept of "too big to fail" should be scrutinized very carefully indeed. I can't help but wonder what would have happened if we had let these "vampire squids" lie where they fell. We are told that the entire economy would have collapsed, but wait a minute; didn't it largely do that anyway? While it is true that many people would have lost a great deal because these firms were holding quite a lot of investment on the part of ordinary people in the form of pension plans, 401Ks, and the like (which had been heavily invested in derivatives), what if we had taken those trillions that we ladled out to the institutions that failed (because, let us not forget, of their greed and recklessness) and given it instead to the people referred to above, who would have lost out? What if we took the people who were defrauded outright by mortgage agencies with Adjustable Rate Mortgages and other loans that the lenders could tell perfectly well the borrowers couldn't possibly repay, and simply gave them the houses on which they had taken out the mortgages, or at least modified their loans so that they could afford them? Really; why not? It seems fair to me; far better than just letting those houses rot as so many of them are now doing. Those who were in the market for purely speculative purposes should go to the end of the repayment line; they should have examined their investments more closely. Repay all retirement funds that would have lost out, and I think there's a real chance that all this would have cost less than what we gave the banksters. Then, let real business needs for real businesses (that are honestly trying to serve human need without gouging people) be served by real banks (create new ones if necessary), community credit unions, and the like. Too big to fail? Just too big; small is beautiful.

It is important to get some sense of how deeply stupid and criminal the activities of the corporados; these self-anointed pillars of our society, have been and how much human suffering has resulted from their activities. We must clear our vision and realize that "by their deeds shall ye know them". Let's just tell it like it is; these are not wise people. They are not good citizens. Regardless of how they strut and preen; regardless of how we allow them to mislead us, when measured on the scale of true humanity they are very small figures. The only thing they can claim to have more of than the rest of us is money and the power derived from that money. They have engaged in criminal behavior on a massive scale, and they have done so deliberately.

They have, as is clearly demonstrated in several of their internal documents, allowed themselves to believe that it is somehow morally acceptable for the one percent to stuff themselves to the point of stupefaction while the ninety-nine percent suffer terribly from these criminals' activities.

Here are a few indicators of how things presently stand with the big dogs; those whom we've come to call the "one percent" (although the really bad actors are actually more like one percent of one percent):

The top one percent have quadrupled their income in the last generation alone; in the first year of the so-called "recovery" they cornered ninety-three percent of the income gains. They now have a greater net worth than the bottom ninety percent of us combined.

Thirty years ago the average CEO made about forty times as much as the average worker; more than fair, wouldn't you think? But now they make two hundred times as much. In 2010 half of Americans earned less than $26,000 per year, while CEOs of the top five hundred corporations got an average of eleven million dollars. Yes, <u>eleven million dollars</u>. Average. Per year.

Meanwhile, as a result of these oligarchs' activities millions of ordinary people have lost homes, jobs, savings, self-esteem, and happiness; even their lives. What would Jesus have to say about that, I wonder? In which connection, I think it's worth pondering the fact that if the real experts [e.g. Jesus] actually knew what they were talking about, 1) we do not cease to exist when we leave this world (more about this later) 2) the state of existence we then experience has as much to do with how we conducted ourselves while we were here as our state today has to do with how we conducted ourselves yesterday ("As ye sow, so shall ye reap.") 3) therefore we do not get away with anything; "every jot and tittle must be paid". How reckless these corporate criminals are, and how ignorant! If they had any idea what they're building for themselves; any real sense of their own long term self-interest, they'd throw it in reverse and put the pedal to the metal. Just as Ebenezer Scrooge eventually did.

Entry-level wages of male high school graduates have fallen twenty-three percent since 1973, and benefits have gone down the drain. Sixty-five percent of high school grads in the private sector received health benefits in 1980; by 2009 only twenty-nine percent did.

Ordinary human beings have to live with the fact that nearly half of the working age people in our nation are now without jobs. There are way too few jobs available to them because so many jobs were shipped overseas by the corporate honchos. Many college graduates now seek in vain for any form of employment, and on top of that they are commonly saddled with huge debts resulting from our society's tolerating for-profit education together with the loan industry that enables it. For those who do have jobs, growth in the rate of inflation has far outstripped wage growth; in desperation, people are taking on crushing debt loads (consumer debt has increased since 1971 by seventeen hundred percent). One out of four American children are now on food stamps.

As the ability of the average American to afford even basic necessities continues to decline, the price of almost everything continues to rise; food, clothing, health care, heating oil, and gasoline, for example. The "American Dream" of material comfort and stability has all but ceased to exist for nearly half of the American people, not just as a present reality but even as a future possibility. For which situation the immediate blame must be put squarely at the door of the corporate oligarchy; the ultimate blame, of course, lies at the feet of the American voter who has allowed all these problems to grow unchecked.

The consequences of such reckless, selfish behavior have been so extreme; the harm that has been done to the American economy (which means to millions of American citizens) is so severe, that sooner or later we will have to take up the question of exactly who was to blame for it all, and why. The debate on this matter has hardly begun, and when really pursued it leads so deep into the labyrinth of human behavior that space precludes an adequate examination here. But I will say that in my opinion the people who enriched themselves so much at such cost to others should have realized from the start that shifting risk from themselves to others in no way got rid of the risk; it just moved it around. The enormous risk associated with, for example, sub-prime mortgage-backed securities was bound to blow up at some point because the original mortgages were doomed to failure; they were sold to people who the mortgage companies knew perfectly well would not be able to pay them off, especially if (which means when) the bubble burst. And it should have been obvious to one and all that allowing credit swaps on a given loan to be sold to others besides the recipient of the loan could only mean that unsustainable obligations would be built up on such loans, as indeed happened so spectacularly when investors flocked to the casino. So once again we have the same sad story; people allowing themselves to be blinded by the lure of money and power, letting the lower angels of our nature control their actions regardless of how harmful those actions turn out to be (and could have been predicted to be with a little thought) for their brothers and sisters who are so easily put out of sight, out of mind, and out of heart.

Astonishingly, we appear to have learned almost nothing from this enormous debacle. These financial giants are bigger and richer than ever. They continue to engage in virtually if not literally all of the practices that caused the financial meltdown that continues to hobble economies around the globe, causing tremendous suffering for millions of people together with the ongoing danger of even worse suffering yet to come. The whole flock of derivatives flies on because it has not been forced to stop and in addition, governments both here and abroad are approaching the problem of our depressed economies in exactly the wrong way, through "austerity" (cutting spending) instead of stimulation (government spending to get things going again, as we did in the Great Depression). It's hard to escape the conclusion that we ain't seen nothin' yet.

POLITICS

How could all this happen? How is it possible for a relatively small number of corporate entities to acquire such power, to use that power in such terribly harmful ways, and to escape unscathed from the conflagration (not just the mess; the situation is ongoing and worsening) they've left behind?

It wasn't only Eisenhower who warned us against turning a blind eye to the activities of those whose chief aim in life was making money regardless of how much harm they caused in the process. Thomas Jefferson was quite clear: "I hope we shall crush in its birth the aristocracy of our moneyed corporations which dare already to challenge our government to a trial of strength and bid defiance to the laws of our country." So was Teddy Roosevelt: "It is necessary that laws should be passed to prohibit the use of corporate funds directly or indirectly for political purposes; it is still more necessary that such laws should be thoroughly enforced." And Franklin Delano Roosevelt: "The liberty of a democracy is not safe if the people tolerate the growth of private power to a point where it becomes stronger than their democratic state itself. That in its essence, is ownership of government by an individual, by a group." Judge Louis Brandeis observed that "We can have democracy in this country, or we can have great wealth concentrated in the hands of a few, but we can't have both." Eugene Debs said "The class which has the power to rob upon a large scale has also the power to control the government and legalize their robbery." And Woody Guthrie: "As through this world you wander you'll meet many funny men. Some will rob you with a six-gun and some with a fountain pen."

How many such statements do we hear from our so-called leaders today? We the people have indeed tolerated "the growth of private power to a point where it becomes stronger than (our) democratic state itself". We have failed to exercise that eternal vigilance that is the price of freedom, and while we slept a terrifying amount of power has gravitated into hands that sought to grasp it. We simply do not any longer have a functioning democracy; we have a corporate oligarchy in which that small group of obscenely wealthy corporados we currently refer to as "the one percent" have nearly absolute control over all three branches of our government together with the media upon which we allow ourselves to depend for information about practically everything (and which lulls us to sleep with an endless stream of meaningless junk and misinformation). That stream of pseudo-information is hugely slanted toward the interests of those who pay for it (regardless of the idiotic myth they push so hard about the "liberal media"), who have no interest whatsoever in communicating important truth to the public, but who have every interest in getting certain ideas into our unresisting heads; ideas which enable them to continue to make enormous amounts of money, just so long as we don't question them, and they're very slick indeed in presenting those ideas; the advertising industry is Machiavellian in its understanding of how to slip things into our so-easily-lulled minds. We're so accustomed to being lied to that we accept it as normal.

For far too long we have been allowing our elected representatives in Congress to make our decisions for us, rather than implementing decisions that we have made. They are not representing our real needs; they don't care about those needs because we don't insist that they care. So they lean with the wind, and that wind blows with great force as an astonishingly large and growing army of lobbyists bends the ears of our senators and representatives; ears that are easily opened by all manner of perks, campaign contributions, and other blandishments furnished by the corporados. Specific legislation is being written by corporate front institutions such as the American Legislative Exchange Council (ALEC) and passed by their puppet congresspeople. And now the so-called Supreme Court (packed with terribly ignorant and unwise people by Geo. W. Bush) has actually, incredibly, possibly fatally to the American Experiment, rendered the Citizens United decision that says that corporations haven't already been given enough freedom to control our elective and legislative processes; that they must be considered "persons" with full enjoyment of all rights conferred upon human beings by the Constitution, e.g. in the First Amendment, which protects free speech, and money is speech!!!

This is simply unbelievable. The highest court in the land has deliberately unleashed the forces of ignorance and greed; it has given them free rein to run absolutely amok in influencing our elections. Your vote and mine now must compete not only with the usual array of political ads and contributions poured forth by corporations to their favored candidates (and usually, to a lesser degree, to the opposition as well; one never can tell) but now with nearly unlimited fundraisers called SuperPACs, which take in enormous amounts of money from terrifically rich people and use it to further the interests of the corporations, not of the public. This kind of thing has been with us as long as politics has, but now it's become tremendously exaggerated and amazingly up front. The most egregious lies are shrugged off as just a normal and necessary part of the electioneering process. Say whatever will get you elected; never mind if has any relation to reality; that doesn't matter. Just keep saying it loud and clear as if it was true, and ignore any statements whatever to the contrary; a substantial portion of the American electorate will believe you because they're so uninformed and unaccustomed to critical thinking; all you have to do is appeal to their emotional prejudices (and make sure they stay away from alternative media). The current leading Republican presidential candidate's staff have openly characterized his presentation of himself as an "etch-a-sketch" whereby one simply erases whatever one said before and replaces it with whatever bilge seems likely to gain supporters in a general election rather than a primary or, it would seem, in any other changing set of conditions. Supposedly astute commentators in all media act as if this was perfectly acceptable; when was the last time you heard one of the Sunday talking heads brace a candidate with a statement like "That's simply absurd! How can you possibly rationalize such a thing? Do you have <u>no</u> understanding of the principles upon which this nation was founded?"

What kind of "democracy" is this? It is not democracy at all; it is in direct opposition to democracy, and if that is not criminal, even treasonous, what is? What could possibly be more harmful to the American Experiment than to cripple its most basic process, whereby the votes of individual citizens are supposed to combine to determine public policy? It is, after all, the ideas; the wishes, the intent of the aggregate of the people, not just of a favored few, that are supposed to determine the actions of our government at every level; federal, state, and local. Government "of, by, and for <u>the people</u>", remember?

In Athens, when they invented democracy they discovered that, as with the Lilliputians and Gulliver, many small people could tie up one large one; a group of citizens overthrew some despotic fool and decided that they'd be better off if they kept power in their own hands. So they gathered in the Forum and had at it, debating issues of importance and coming up with decisions about what to do. And one of the first things that they decided was the primary importance of one principle; <u>they were not selecting representatives to make decisions for the people, but to implement the decisions that the people had made</u>. These representatives were supposed to be figuring out the best ways to implement the will of the people, who made the decisions expressing that will by and for themselves.

Since provincial times, in the towns of early America the citizens would gather to debate and decide all matters of significant importance to their community; to this day they still have Town Meetings in New England for the same purpose. The dominant characteristic of these activities was consensus. It was considered to be of paramount importance that all points of view were heard and that all minorities understood that their position had been openly and genuinely considered so that they would be content, if not pleased with decisions with which they did not agree. This was easily understandable in that at that time the nation consisted mostly of small towns with an agrarian economic base. Everyone knew everyone else, and they all realized that harmony within the community was essential to the continuation of the town's existence. And another very important thing; it was considered quite improper to seek office; to campaign for any position, because people were chosen by the town, of (from the citizenry of) the town, and for the town; they were expected to act not in favor of any special interest but in the interest of the town as a whole. They were selected to serve the public interest, not to personally aggrandize or enrich themselves.

Gradually, however, special interests did develop as they have throughout human history. People actively sought the power of public office not primarily for the general good but for limited purposes in which they had a personal interest. Much ale was spread around in the taverns; in fact, the tavern owner became something of a power broker. And so began the seemingly inevitable process of power gravitating into hands that sought to grasp it.

Today in our nation (and not, of course, only in ours) the norm, or regrettably close to it, seems to have become to accept as a serious candidate for office whatever quacking fool has the advisers that best know how to tell us what we want to hear (and what we want to hear has been largely formed by an endless stream of corporate propaganda on TV, the internet, and what print media still exist); they know that we have almost completely lost the desire or the ability to seriously question whether or not this guy or gal <u>will</u> actually fix the economy, stop "terrorism", repair the roads, or any of the other things they so glibly promise to do. We seem to have almost no capacity for critical thinking; we're perfectly happy to take the words for the deeds. So we get the kind of election campaign that we've seen in the current Presidential campaign year, in which a pack of amazingly ignorant and thoughtless people bleat and bloviate away about next to nothing of any real importance, pretending that they're actually viable candidates for the Presidency of the United States. It's an astonishing display that would be absolutely hilarious if it wasn't so serious, not only in what it says about the candidates but in what it says about us. How can we possibly allow ourselves to believe that these people are legitimate candidates? Because for one thing the media treats them as if they were, when they should be exposing them for what they are. Week in and week out, the talking heads, pundits, whatever, continue to lob softballs at these foolish people, pretending that the truth always lies halfway between opposing views that must be accorded equal respect; almost never do they bore in and confront them with any of the countless questions that would show who they really are. And we lap it up as if it was real. Like what they call "reality shows" on TV, that have virtually no resemblance to reality. Shame on them; shame on us.

There are people out there, plenty of them, who are qualified to be real, effective representatives of the citizens of the United States. But they generally don't run for office because they know perfectly well that they'll be up against a financial juggernaut that supports candidates who aren't interested in the reality of normal people's lives; these candidates, while uttering all sorts of pretty words (along with amazingly ugly ones that we seem to let roll right off our backs), are not interested in the welfare of the common people; they're interested in the wishes of their corporate masters, and they know that they have to kowtow to these people in order to have a chance of getting elected, because it now takes enormous amounts of money to get elected and they are the ones with the money. Once in a while some hero or heroine will give it a go and actually take office, but the odds are hugely against their being able to accomplish much in Congress because they're such a tiny minority. All this is somehow accepted, both by Congress and by the public. All kinds of insane things are accepted; things like "riders", where some Congressperson's pet project of the moment (most likely some rich donor's pet project) is grafted onto a bill that has nothing to do with it, but which seems sure of passing. The rider just goes along with it. Say <u>what</u>? Aren't they supposed to take each project by itself, discuss it specifically, and decide its fate on its merits alone? Or how about the amazing situation in the House of Representatives wherein Democratic Representatives can't even vote on a bill if a majority of the Republicans (who control the House because they're in the majority) don't agree that they (the Republicans) have the votes to pass or defeat the bill?! Is there no limit to the nonsense we will allow?

As we all know, our Congress has now become so fractious and uninterested in reality that they are nearly paralyzed. And this mess has been brought about primarily by the Republicans, who have lost, evidently along with their hearts and minds, virtually all sense of what America is really supposed to be about; who think that Jesus requires that we smite the godless Muslim (a central tenet of Islam is "There is no God but God") or anyone else that our now-massive national insecurity system deems to be a potential "terrorist"; that poor people are poor only because they're lazy; that women have no right to make vital decisions regarding their own lives, that a health care system that conforms to the most basic requirements of common decency is socialism (a terrible thing, as we all know); that the natural cycle of climate change hasn't been affected by human activities and that the current state of that cycle is perfectly OK; that rich people should pay very low taxes and should get enormous government handouts so that they can make even more money; that in order to protect ourselves from those who fill us with terror we must give up the most precious freedoms upon which this nation was based (we were so terrorized by 9/11 that we willingly gave up some of our most important freedoms, through such horrendously fearful and un-American legislation as the Patriot act and the National Defense Authorization Act); and on and on and on. Since the administration of George W. Bush and Dick Cheney the "neo-cons" have acted with such ignorance, short-sightedness, mendacity, and utter heartlessness that the mind reels to contemplate it.

This situation has been not only tolerated but furthered by the Democrats as well, who since the sixties seem to have been able to conceive of little better than to try weakly to copy the Republicans (with Carter as a strong exception and Clinton as a weaker one, along with a few fine legislators; they know who they are). Granted, they're not nearly as good at it as the Republicans because they do still have a weak but discernible heart, and they do occasionally show small flashes of actual intelligence. But they've become worse than useless; they're deeply complicit in one of the greatest crimes that humanity has ever experienced; the near-ruining of the American Experiment by allowing the will of the people to be supplanted by the will of a corporate oligarchy.

The current state of affairs in Congress has been aptly described by a member of the British press as "a colossal collective abdication of responsibility by the people's elected representatives". But the key word here is "elected"; all this has been tolerated by us; "we the people" who when all is said and done are responsible for the behavior of our government. We have been perfectly willing to hide our heads in the sand as things went from bad to worse, allowing the power of our vote to slip away and pretending that there was nothing we could do about it; besides, who cares? I really don't matter. Only one vote, after all, right? Don't I have enough to worry about, just trying to get by and have a little fun? We elect those people to take care of all this; if they can't do it how can I? I work all day doing something I'd much prefer not to have to do (which is why we're addicted to lotteries), because I'll die if I don't. In fact, I'll die anyway; what a deal! What I need at the end of the day is a beer and a cop show. Don't bother me with politics.

Nonetheless, large numbers of us have begun to realize that things are not going well, and two very significant movements have arisen as a result. But these movements have very different views as to the causes of and the solutions for this situation; as a result of this division the movements functionally oppose each other.

The first of these movements to grow to a position of significant influence is the Tea Party, which formed when a large number of people agreed that their government was not meeting their needs. Unfortunately, this was interpreted to be a result of intrinsic flaws in government per se, and the solution was to basically do away with government. This feeling was nicely expressed by a figure of enormously excessive influence who said "Shrink government to where it will fit in a bathtub and then drown it!" Such an attitude is spectacularly ignorant of the rightful, necessary functions of government; functions which have been the proper role of governments ever since they were invented, and of which we are presently in desperate need. It is shockingly simplistic. It lacks the intelligence to think with any depth about either the problem or the solution. The Tea Party seems to be utterly unable to see that the enemy is not government itself but the takeover and abuse of one of the best governments that ever existed, by a corporate oligarchy. The result of this regrettably limited view has been that the Tea Party has become little more than a branch of the far-right Republican Party, which has clearly demonstrated that it is perfectly willing to shut down government, or at least to cripple its functioning. The Tea Party has thus become far more a part of the problem than of the solution, playing right into the hands of the worst corporate marionettes in Congress. Never have I seen a better example of the fact that a little knowledge is a dangerous thing, and this is especially tragic because if only the Tea Party folks could be a little more intelligent and educated, they would realize that their concerns coincide remarkably well with the second group; the Occupy Movement.

The Occupy Movement is by far the most hopeful development of recent years, indeed decades. Things have gotten so bad; the condition of not just our economy but of our environment, our politics, and virtually every other important area of public life has deteriorated so alarmingly that a very large number of people who are thinking intelligently and who are aware of the facts regarding our current state of affairs, have begun to come together to share their dissatisfaction and to see what can be done about it. They are going about this in a fascinating way, employing truly democratic principles and attempting to be as inclusive as possible, with the result that a wonderful variety of people are becoming involved. It remains to be seen how this energy can be translated into meaningful action; they are facing an immense uphill fight and they know it.

One thing that could be greatly helpful would be if the Occupy Movement could get together with the Tea Party folks in recognition of their common interest. That would truly be a force to reckon with, but it presupposes that the Tea Party can muster the courage and vision to see their fundamental error in attacking our government rather than those who have so abused it. But that, sadly, does not seem likely. So all in all, the task is enormous. Not for the faint of heart.

What can we to to fix this situation? Is it too late to save ourselves? Of course not; we still have democratic systems in place. All we have to do is use them, but we must do so intelligently and with heart rather than behaving with our usual ignorance. There is no way around it; we now <u>must</u> get involved if we are to rescue the American Experiment. And that means that we must become politically aware; to see through the sham that characterizes most political activity and to take the necessary steps to fix the situation. The best way to become aware is to listen to those on both sides of the conservative/liberal chasm we have allowed to separate us from each other; to really listen and to learn. Both sides have real concerns; it's time that we learned what they are. If we do this we will see clearly that our central problem is not each other; it is the theft of our democracy by the corporate oligarchy. We will realize that nearly all of the multiple crises into which we have allowed ourselves to drift are the direct result of the activities of that oligarchy, and that if we hope to deal effectively with any of these crises we must first address the central problem that is common to them all. It is not a question of blame or punishment but simply of facing the facts; we have been allowing children to play with matches. They have nearly burned down the house and it's time that we put a stop to it.

The only way that I can see to do this is to force Congress to pass a Constitutional amendment that completely does away with the absurd notion of corporate personhood, but which goes much further than that. Halfway measures cannot work; power will go right back to the corporate monster unless we drive a stake through its heart. Such an amendment must prohibit, once and for all, any corporate influence in our elective or legislative processes. Hands off! These affairs are the province of we the people; all the people, not the one percent. Every corporate executive gets one vote, just like the rest of us. No more and no less; no lobbyists, no perks, no American Legislative Exchange Council corporate lackeys writing legislation, no campaign contributions (all political campaigns should be government-financed, with equal resources available to every serious candidate). And it would be an excellent idea, in view of the fact that every corporation is incorporated with a specific charter, to go back to something we used to do before the corporados stood democracy on its head; require every corporation to undergo a periodic review by an independent panel of citizens. If that panel determines that a given corporation is not serving the public interest then its charter is revoked. No more, ever, of this nonsense about "too big to fail". A fine example of such a thorough and potentially effective amendment can be seen in the Network of Spiritual Progressives' Environmental and Social Responsibility Act; check it out at spiritualprogressives.org. And get a dose of hope while you're at it.

What if we actually do get our democracy back, tuned up, and functioning properly? We must consider what we can look forward to if and when we get the American Experiment to function as it was intended to. Is our goal to simply stabilize our economy; to have the Dow stay forever over thirteen thousand, to have adequate food, clothing, and shelter, together with a nearly infinite variety of entertainment to distract us from the really important things in life? Or, perhaps, is there something better than that in store for us once we get our house in order? Something that will benefit each and every one of us beyond what we can yet imagine? Something that some of our wisest people have always said was at the heart of the American Experiment, waiting for us to become aware of and to put into practice? Part Two of this little diatribe will attempt to explore these questions.

RELIGION

From the days of the Puritans, religion has played a vital role in our nation's affairs. Very few of us yet understand much about life, death, or any other fundamental reality. We move ahead as best we can in the face of the central, undeniable fact that at some point for each of us the whole show will seemingly inevitably come to an end. That idea horrifies us (as it should; we'll get to that later) and we need reassurance.

We look to our religions for that comfort. The extraordinary figures who inspired the great religions seem to stand out in their understanding of the human condition and of the greater reality within which that condition exists. We are comforted by their words. But we make one enormous mistake; we worship these individuals instead of worshiping the truth that they tried to get us to see and understand. We do this because we seem to have been incapable of thinking deeply about what those remarkable people tried to tell us, and make no mistake; the intent of the best of them was for us to think very deeply indeed about these things in order that we come into the heritage of personal understanding that is our destiny. Jesus, for instance, said "Why do you call <u>me</u> holy?" "Of myself I can do nothing." ("The father within doeth the work.") "The Kingdom of Heaven is within you." And "These things and more shall <u>ye</u> do." Isn't it obvious that he intended for us not to worship him but to copy him? And he, along with our other great spiritual teachers, told us a great deal about how to do that.

We have failed to understand this central truth. Instead of delving deeply into our religious beliefs and thus coming to understand the greater realities to which they open us, we close off; we cling to our beliefs. Because really, when you come right down to it, unquestioned and uninvestigated they remain essentially <u>beliefs</u>, not knowledge in which we can rest secure. Whenever they are questioned we feel threatened, to the exact extent of the desperation with which we cling to them. We set ourselves against each other according to the differences in our religious beliefs, and we have historically been perfectly willing to slaughter each other mercilessly in the belief that we are defending our faith, on the strange assumption that it or any other faith needs defending (why can't we just shrug our shoulders and say "Each of us believes what he or she believes"?). We evangelize furiously; since we refuse to question our own beliefs, as good teachers always insist we do, we instead seek strength in numbers; the more people we can convert to our way of looking at things, the better. Misery loves company.

In keeping with the above tendency we in this nation have, throughout our history but particularly significantly in the last fifty years or so, mixed religion very strongly with politics, in spite of our professed separation of church and state. The theory here is that they really shouldn't be separated because without religion (<u>our</u> religion, of course), the activities of state will be grounded in essentially heathen principles (obviously not necessarily true if one thinks about it, no matter what your religion may be). So we have seen highly motivated and very active religious groups (evangelical Christians) working their way into politics, starting with Ronald Reagan and culminating with George W. Bush's presidency. High powered evangelists gained extraordinary access to the White House and the halls of Congress, and they have had a very strong influence on the attitudes and actions of all three branches of government and the media as well. Unfortunately, their influence has been almost exclusively negative and harmful to the interests of the general public, primarily because these evangelists have been terribly uninformed about what has really been going on on this planet, and also because they have been, like the rest of us, nearly devoid of the capacity to exercise critical thinking.

There is a huge irony here in that these people's chief fault has been not just in failing to see how wrong they were in certain ways, but in not realizing how and in what ways they have been <u>right</u> all along. Their fundamental need for security is the same as, and just as justifiable as anyone else's. Their intuitive sense of the reality of God is absolutely correct. Their specific concerns about such things as the sanctity of human life are grounded in reality. But they haven't been secure in these understandings because they haven't penetrated deeply enough into any of them; they haven't realized that the only real security comes from deep personal understanding, not from just saying nice things or clinging to comfortable beliefs furnished by somebody else.

Many of us have become aware of these unfortunate realities, but we must not make the mistake of throwing out the baby with the bathwater in the case of our religions or of our government. What we must now do is come to understand the great truths that underly both of these entities; they have been carrying around humanity's blue chips, which we have known intuitively are valuable but which we haven't learned how to cash in. Things have evolved on this planet, however much it might seem otherwise. These blue chips; the deep truths that our religions and our democratic system have always preserved for us, are now accessible to us. It's time that we learned how to cash them. In that effort we would do well to bear in mind the Theosophists' wonderful motto: "There is no religion higher than Truth".

CURRENT EVENTS

Almost everyone on earth now realizes that a lot is happening in human affairs and in the effects that those affairs have upon the natural systems of our planet. Almost everything that appears in the corporate media is negative; wars, rumors of wars, earthquakes, monsoons, floods, tsunamis, fire, economic disaster, nuclear disaster, political chaos, and on and on and on. What is happening is that the chickens are coming home to roost; we are seeing the results of having behaved the way we have chosen to accept as normal (and thus made it so); this behavior has consisted primarily of whatever groups of humans happen to have acquired power using that power for their own short-sighted and selfish ends, utterly heedless of the effects of that behavior upon their fellow human beings or the planet itself. You can only do this kind of thing so long before you reap the inevitable consequences, which are now cascading down upon our heads. It remains to be seen how terrible these consequences have to be before we wake up and realize that we're being forced to choose once and for all between Right and Wrong, but that's what's happening, and we'd better get the message pretty soon or we'll destroy our life on this earth.

So serious is our current state of affairs, so terribly costly in terms of human suffering, so frightening in its implications if not properly addressed, that the reality of the situation is becoming apparent to a rapidly increasing number of people, as best exemplified by the Occupy Movement. Most of these people are young, not yet having been corrupted by the normal "nothing I can do about it" routines of a lifetime spent "on the job"; a shockingly large number of them can't get a job anyway, even with a college education, because there just aren't that many jobs available any more, even flipping burgers. One might think that this would be the natural result of the corporados having shut down factory after factory in this country so that they could take advantage of much cheaper labor costs in other countries, and one would be right.

The American economy fell off a cliff in 2008, and it did so with blinding speed; one week things were more or less normal, the next we were told that our entire economy was in immediate danger of total collapse, unless we, the victims of the wretched scam, coughed up literally trillions of dollars on top of everything else we'd lost or were about to lose, to bail out the very villains who caused the whole mess! Absolutely unbelievable, until one realizes that the corporados control the government. President Obama, who came into office sounding as though he really understood some of the basic dynamics in play and would actually attempt to do something about it, surrounded himself with people drawn from the very cast of characters responsible for the debacle. No surprise, therefore, that the thrust of our government's efforts to deal with the problem focused on shoring up the perpetrators rather than assisting their victims in any meaningful way. Because they were "too big to fail". Simply shameful. Any institution too big to fail (what on earth could that mean?) is simply too big, and should be disbanded in the public interest. No loss to the public; only to the billionaires. These vampire squids, as someone so aptly called them, should have been left to rot and then been recycled into something of benefit to the human race. If we need banks, let's use the real ones; the community credit unions and local banks who do honest banking, and get rid of these ruinous criminal enterprises that masquerade as responsible social entities while they ruin the lives of millions, serving the interests of the super rich.

Our core problem, with which we must now deal, is the takeover of our democracy by a corporate oligarchy that has so seriously impacted so many areas of our lives that it must be stopped in its tracks and its power must be taken away once and for all if we are to avoid disaster on a scale that would be in nobody's interest. If we can free ourselves from the grip of the corporate monster, and from our own mentality that caused us to abdicate our democratic responsibilities and to thus allow that monster to threaten the entire American Experiment, then here is a bit more of what we can expect to discover when we begin to care about discovering it:

PART TWO

THE FUTURE

"The preservation of the sacred fire of liberty…(is) justly considered as staked deeply, <u>perhaps as finally</u> (emphasis added) upon the experiment entrusted to the hands of the American people." (George Washington)

"…the <u>last</u> (emphasis added), best hope of earth." (Abraham Lincoln)

"Liberty of searching out truth is hardly got and as hardly kept; we must part with lands and life before parting with such a jewel." (Roger Williams)

We should keep in mind that in the last analysis nobody is to be blamed for what has happened. God loves each of us equally; so should we love one another. We must realize that each of us is doing the best we can, whether we are fortunate enough to see this world as filled with beauty and promise, or whether we are unfortunate enough to see it as a dog-eat-dog affair where only the strong survive. Our behavior, whether as individuals or as groups, proceeds directly from how well or how poorly we understand the real facts of life, and it's about time that we learned these basic facts. It's time that we realized, for example, that no human being is our enemy. The common enemies of all mankind are fear, greed, and the ignorance from which they both proceed, and the weapons that will defeat them are faith, love, and understanding.

There is nothing new in the behavior of our corporado brothers and sisters. They have simply been yielding to the lower angels of their nature rather than the higher ones, and who of us throughout human history has not done the same in one way or another; indeed, who does not do so daily? The unenlightened idea that one person is better than another simply because they have more money (or power; they have become nearly synonymous) has always been with us, whether in the special privileges of kings or in the social Darwinism that has poisoned our history for well over a century. But it is inherently dehumanizing; it has led historically to shocking conditions in the way employees have been treated by their employers, ranging in this country from the inhuman conditions of the Lowell textile mills to the murderous thuggery of Henry Ford's anti-union forces. And make no mistake; it continues today in a wide variety of conditions that, so often as to be typical, reduce the condition of the average worker to a state of wage slavery. Nonetheless, we would do well to bear in mind the old saying "The Lord loves a sinner" because when serious sinners come around they do so with all that energy and expertise. If and when our corporado siblings wake up and fly right, they can become a tremendous force for good; there are so many good things being done, with literally infinite opportunities to do more! So many people are working to make the world a better place, whether helping their brothers and sisters in need, making astonishing scientific discoveries, inventing incredibly creative and wonderful things, creating art of all kinds, increasing our understanding of important realities, and on and on. With so much good to do and so much satisfaction to be gained from doing it, why on earth would we waste our precious time doing bad things?

The attitude that any one of us is fundamentally better than any other is and has always been simply ignorant. There is an old spiritual saying: "The only sin is ignorance." If we knew the truth we could not possibly behave the way we do. But unfortunately, we have never had much real understanding of what we're doing in this world. As we have observed, we don't know what we are, where we come from, where we're going, or what's going on, and we don't try to know because it is generally assumed that we can't know. But now this can and must change; we must open to the real, unimaginably wonderful truth of all these things, and the first step is to realize that we <u>can</u> "search out truth", through the proper use of our bodily senses, our minds, and most importantly, our hearts.

For the purposes of this discussion we can say that there are two distinct areas of life; the material and the spiritual. The way we explore the former is with our mind; with the latter we become concerned with values, not just facts, so we must also use that vital internal faculty that we call our hearts. But in order for this exploration to succeed we must use these faculties properly, not in the regrettably undisciplined and slipshod manner to which we seem to be accustomed.

When we fail to see any thing as it really is, it is essential that we be able to think critically about that thing; to observe the facts relating to it and to compare those facts in a rational and objective way. In order to do that we must be free from any undue outer or inner influence, whether positive blandishments or negative threats; either one will distort our view and make it impossible for us to see clearly. It is equally important that we be open to the truth, whatever that truth may turn out to be. In short, in order to find Truth we have to be serious about it; it is not too much to say that we must worship Truth in order to find it. And it is also true that when we do earnestly seek Truth, we do begin to find it.

The rules for using our minds successfully are 1) Choose our premises objectively, not as a result of our emotional preferences, either positive or negative, and 2) Think about those premises rationally, or logically. Here is where precise definition seems to become impossible. I've been searching through my best dictionaries for a clear definition of rationality and logic, and what it seems to boil down to is that they're virtually synonymous; logic being "the science of reasoning" (rationality), or "the correct way to think". In other words, the discipline of thinking in a way that works; that leads to an increased perception of the truth of the matter in hand. Logic is recognized as the "correct" way because it works; the entire cosmos is logically put together, so logical thought upon correct premises will lead to increased awareness of reality. For now, with our skill in logical thought being in its current relatively low state we will simply have to do our best, realizing that our skill will improve, as will the results of our efforts. We just have to try to be reasonable; to practice the way of thinking that realizes that if two twos equal four, and two fours equal eight, then four twos must equal eight.

In spiritual matters it is our heart that tells us the truth, but again, we must learn to use our hearts properly, not confusing the feelings of our heart with our emotions. It is our heart, not our mind that tells us that right is RIGHT and wrong is WRONG; that love is good and hate is bad; that we should help rather than hurt each other. Our hearts tell us what is real justice; what is fair, what is kind, what is loving. And these are truly the most important matters with which we have to deal; the standards by which successful life must be lived. Understanding these things is entirely a matter of <u>feeling</u>, not of thinking. While it is true that we can rationally figure out the facts of any given subject, it is with our hearts that we discern the deeper meaning of those facts. The mind can lead the horse to water but it is with the heart that we drink.

As we seriously pursue Truth, one of the most helpful things we can do is to share our thoughts with each other rather than jealously defending them against what we perceive as an attack whenever someone questions them. The perfect analogy here is that old one about the blind men and the elephant, where one man has the elephant by the tail and thus perceives it as being like a broom; he can feel the handle and count the bristles. The second man has it by the leg; he sees it as just like a tree; he can feel the bark. When the first man says that the thing is like a broom, the second man says "Like hell it is! It's like a tree!" And we have war (with nobody saying anything that isn't true!). Well, wouldn't it be better to assume that each of us has reasons for saying what we do, and to inquire as to what those reasons might be? That way we could learn from each other rather than fighting each other. Imagine how much better off we would be if we were to open to each other in this way, rather than closing off and shutting each other out, thus losing the benefit of what any of us knows that any other does not.

Throughout the history of the human race we have been subjected to an astonishing variety of influences that have prevented us from discovering the most basic facts about our existence, our purpose here, or anything else of real importance. We have always been preoccupied with the struggle for food, clothing, shelter, and everything else we feel that we need or want. Most of us spend our day doing something we would much prefer not to do, because we seem to have no choice; we will die if we don't face the "hard, cold facts" of life. Who can blame us for trying to fill whatever free time we can get with fun, not politics or philosophy?

But we don't learn much that way. We live in substantial ignorance of what's going on around us, including a great deal that will affect us very significantly (such as, for example, climate change, mortgage fraud, political chicanery at every level or for that matter, death). We choose to stay ignorant, so we make it easy for power to gravitate into hands that seek to grasp it, and that power is almost invariably used primarily for the perceived self-interest of whoever wields it, not for the common good. The average guy plods on as best he can, hoping for the best but far too often finding the worst. Neither we nor those who have accumulated power over us have the slightest idea of what we're doing. As observed above, we don't know what we are, where we come from, where we're going, or what's going on; quite a handicap, as we had better come to realize.

The way things have always worked is that since the average person has no interest in seeking power, power gravitates easily into the hands that do seek it. Humans originally gathered into groups that were, until the rise of the nation-state, comparatively small, and these groups competed with each other as animals generally do, almost solely on the basis of the biggest dog getting the bone. Then, when things had evolved into a situation where large nations existed with great power, comparatively small interest groups began to acquire power over the doings of these nations; now we have a miniscule fraction of the population controlling the affairs of nearly all the nations of the world. Their activities have not just ignored the common good; they have worked directly against it, to the point where these activities are now actually threatening to breach the narrow natural boundaries within which life as we know it can exist.

But we in the United States of America live in a very special situation. We have a nation that has been blessed with stunning material resources and we have systems in place which, if only we would wake up and understand them, are designed to put those resources to use for the benefit of the entire human race in its journey toward its actual destiny. Those systems (democracy and free enterprise) are specifically designed to free the individual from the pressures that distort our ability to see things as they are.

Almost anyone can see that the great appeal of this nation to the rest of the world has always been summed up in the word "freedom". That means, of course, freedom from being subject to the whims of a lord, a dictator, or anyone else, together with the freedom to make a living by whatever means we choose, but a far more important issue is what we are supposed to do with that freedom above and beyond just meeting the material necessities of life. To date, the best we seem to have been able to come up with is the idea that we have to be free to make as much money as possible, but that is that is far from the highest and best use of our freedom. George Washington's "American Experiment" was intended to be very much more important than that; it was intended to demonstrate that the average human being had and would exercise, if free to do so, the capacity and the will to seek out the meaning of life and thus to live meaningfully, happily, and profitably in the highest sense.

This vision of the nature and high importance of the American Experiment existed (although by no means generally) from the very beginning of this nation, in the early days of the Massachusetts Bay Colony, where in 1630 (ten years after the Mayflower landed) there appeared one Roger Williams, an ecclesiastic and visionary who had found it prudent to escape the same turmoil in England that had forced the Puritans out. He was well thought of, so much so that upon arrival he was offered the job of "teacher" in the Boston church; about as elevated a job as could be found at the time. But he turned them down because, as he vigorously and continually informed them, they were not allowing freedom of the individual at all, nor were they separating church from state, and he would have none of such doings.

The Massachusetts Bay Colony was in fact a stone-cold theocracy. You could have a hole burned in your tongue or your ears cropped (or worse, as Mary Dyer and several others found out) if you didn't toe the line with respect to either religious or secular orthodoxy, both of which were inextricably entwined. They didn't just give democracy short shrift, they wanted no part of it. "Democracy is amongst civil nations, accounted the meanest and worst of all forms of government…a manifest breach of the fifth commandment." (John Winthrop, Governor of Massachusetts Bay Colony) "Democracy, I do not conceive that ever God did ordain as a fit government either for church or commonwealth. If the people be governors who shall be governed?" (John Cotton, MBC high preacher) Really. No kidding! The Good Old Pilgrims.

Williams refused to change his ways; he wouldn't shut up, and eventually he was driven out by the MBC leaders in the middle of a howling blizzard that would very likely have killed him had he not been, almost uniquely among the colonists, in good standing with the Indians (three of whose languages he learned), who took him in and saved his life. He then went on to found his own colony, in a place he called "Providence" (which became Rhode Island), where he enshrined the principles of freedom of individual conscience and absolute separation of church and state. We commonly associate these principles with the "Founding Fathers" like Jefferson, Madison, Paine, et al, but it was Roger Williams who approximately a hundred and forty years earlier, alone and in the face of potentially lethal opposition, insisted that practicing, not just preaching these principles constituted the heart of what our doings in this new land should be about. I consider him to be the Founding Father.

Williams was quite clear on this point; he realized that the real purpose of freedom of the individual was not fundamentally a material matter but a spiritual one. "Liberty of searching out truth is hardly got and as hardly kept; we must part with lands and life before parting with such a jewel." "Searching out truth"; this was the highest and best use of the enormous resources that this new land offered; the support of the individual human being in his/her search for the real Truth of things. Its highest purpose was not concerned with food, clothing, or shelter but with, as Williams put it, "the eternal felicity of man". Here is a wonderful quote from my favorite biography of Williams; "Roger Williams, New England Firebrand" by James Ernst who, unlike many of Williams's other chroniclers, was capable of understanding where Williams was really coming from: "The Seekerism of Roger Williams is his spiritual journey into the unknown in quest of the realization of his immortal self--his soul--, broadening his consciousness, seeking a higher and higher unity, ever striving to approach nearer to the one central Truth which is all-comprehensive. This journey and quest is also the central fact in the history of mankind."

It is of critical importance now for us to understand this, because of the nature of the enormous shift that is currently under way on this planet. We are in the early stages of our fourth quantum evolutionary shift, from what is called the Fourth Kingdom to the Fifth. We have had three such shifts already, from the "mineral kingdom" to the vegetable, from vegetable to animal, and from animal to human (although I think "proto-human" might be more accurate; we have a way to go before we can really call ourselves human). Each of these shifts was what we could call "quantum", meaning that it involved not just newness but a new kind of newness. The difference between a rock and a plant is quantum in this sense of the word. So is the difference between a plant and an animal, and that between other animals and the human animal. And what we are about to become will be at least equally different from what we perceive ourselves to be now. And just as much of an advance; just as wonderful.

As we have already observed, there is a vitally important thing to understand about the coming evolutionary shift that is completely new. Always before, each life form has had no choice whatever in the shift to a new form but this time the shift will be entirely dependent upon the understanding and conscious choice of the individual human being to actively participate in this change. This is why it is so important for each of us to understand what is going on; to be able to think clearly about it and what it involves and implies and, most importantly, to <u>feel</u> the value of it. And that in turn makes the success of the American Experiment tremendously significant, not just for the well-being of the nation but for the betterment of humanity as a whole, because that individual enlightenment is what the American Experiment is all about.

THE FIFTH KINGDOM

What can we expect as we look ahead with the new evolutionary shift in mind? Will we be moving into a state of affairs where we can run our cars on water? Where everyone will be rich and able to buy whatever suits their fancy? Where our major material problems are solved and our day-to-day life is easy and enjoyable? Possibly any or all of the above, but the thing to see is that we can expect not just material improvements but far more important, a radical expansion of our view of life itself and our place in it. We are in a very similar position to that of the chick as it begins to peck its way out of the egg into an entirely new world (which it does of necessity, being out of food and space).

Here are four examples of the things we will be coming to understand, and the understanding of which will allow us to escape from the prison in which up to now we have been willing to exist. We should bear in mind that this understanding will require real openness, critical thinking, and strong hearts. Each of us must learn to feel the importance of these things and to think them through to the point where we see the truth by and for ourselves. So let's consider the following things that we must and will come to understand:

1) What God Is

The word "God" has several definitions, but almost invariably these definitions are basically imaginary; images created in our minds, generally featuring an exceedingly wise old graybeard on a cloud or streets of gold somewhere; in fact, an imaginary figure created in our own image. That image is obviously an important and extremely useful one, representing as it does our intuitive understanding that something of immense power, beauty, and mystery must have put us (and everything else) here, but it is still just an image; we need to be clear about exactly what reality that image is supposed to represent. Clearly, this anthropomorphic image is insufficient for the needs of our time, when we have drifted so far from the truth that we are in real danger of ruining the ability of life as we know it to continue on this planet; when instead of understanding, obeying, and loving God we habitually tear each other to pieces over our differing religious views.

What the word "God" refers to in the minds of the wisest among us is simply this: "That Which Created Everything". By the law of conservation of energy, no thing can come from nothing because there can be no such thing as nothing. Therefore we can see with certainty that something (not some <u>thing</u> but <u>something</u>) must have created all of creation, and we call that "something" God. We have a tremendous barrier to real understanding of this essential, simple, and self-evident fact in that most of us just don't feel the reality of anything unless it can be perceived by one or more of our five physical senses. We commonly refer to the material world (that which is perceptible to our physical senses) as "the real world" in spite of the fact that our physical senses only perceive a tiny sliver of material reality; anything else seems unreal. We almost completely ignore anything that we can't see, hear, smell, touch, or feel with our body. But what about ideas? Our idea of, say, an automobile is just as real as the automobile itself; it's just a different reality, just as a photograph and the scene it portrays are both real but quite different. Ideas <u>are</u> photographs; pictures of realities that the idea represents. And in spite of the fact that they are not "solid", we certainly consider them to be real; we use them all the time. So when you think about it, we really are quite well acquainted with the reality of what isn't "solid".

There is a wonderful Biblical phrase "the substance of things unseen". This states the case beautifully; there is no such thing as nothing but there most definitely is such a thing as "not-thingness", out of which all thingness arose, and the name we give to this fundamental creative reality is "God". We must now come to fully realize that beyond all material reality is that which created that reality, and it must be just as real as that which it created; it must have "substance".

Here is another thought to ponder; what did God have to make anything out of when the creative process began? Only God; there was (and is, and never can be) anything else but God, manifesting in all the wondrous, kaleidoscopic forms that evolution has produced. Therefore every created thing is literally God manifesting <u>as that thing</u>, and the human creature is the only creature we know of that has the capacity to see itself in that light. And by the way, for those who have trouble with the concept of evolution; the word simply refers to the growth of the plant that is life on earth, as it goes through the miraculous transformative process of arising out of a seed, developing a shoot, a stem, leaves, and then a blossom (and if that isn't "intelligent design" what is?). And we, the human creature, are the bud in that plant; we are beginning to open out into a blossom. Beyond that, who knows?

So God is That Which Created It All, and everything that God created is literally a form of God. We can go ahead and use the word now, understanding clearly what it refers to. But obviously we can't call God "He" or "She" any more, can we? We'll just have to say "God" a lot (or "Jehovah", or "Allah", or whatever we prefer; I cannot believe that our Creator cares what word we use). And that won't hurt us a bit.

2) What Faith is

We hear the word "faith" fairly often, generally in the context of being asked to trust someone or something. But trust is often problematic; how many times have we put our trust in a person or a situation, or a thing, only to be terribly disappointed? What we want to learn is how to trust people to do what they <u>do</u>, not what we'd like to believe they will do; to trust situations to yield the results that they really <u>will</u> yield, not what we wishfully believe they will. In short, we need to be realistic; to learn where we can and cannot place our trust.

The highest octave of faith is trust in God; most of us realize that to a degree but not so many of us understand what it really means. First of all, we must see that God is totally, absolutely, eternally worthy of our full trust. God does not make mistakes. God does not play practical jokes. God NEVER punishes us for anything (more on this later). So what does it mean to have faith in God?

Let an expert speak to the matter: "Take therefore no thought for your life, what ye shall eat; neither for the body, what ye shall put on...Consider the lilies how they grow; they toil not, they spin not; and yet I say unto you, that Solomon in all his glory was not arrayed like one of these. If God so clothed the grass... how much more will he clothe you, oh ye of little faith? And seek not what ye shall eat, or what ye shall drink, neither be ye of doubtful mind. For...your Father knoweth that ye have need of these things. But rather seek ye the kingdom of God; and all these things shall be added unto you. Fear not, little flock; for it is your Father's good pleasure to give you the kingdom."

What Jesus is saying here (Luke 12: 22-32) is so simple that it generally eludes us. "Seek ye the kingdom of God" and we'll have everything we need. Don't worry about any of it. This seems so contradictory to the facts of life as we have always known them that it hardly seems worthy of a moment's attention. At no time in human history has it generally seemed realistic to think that we could get food in our mouths by just wishing for it; there is a wonderful Chinese saying: "A peasant will stand on a hill for a long time with his mouth open before a roast duck flies in."

It is important to understand that God providing for us does not mean that God will do for us anything that we should be doing for ourselves; what it does mean is that we will be guaranteed everything we need (starting with a body and a place to put it) to do what we should be doing. And "what we should be doing" also turns out to be utterly simple; it means "what we <u>love</u> to do". Not just what we "like"; we can like all sorts of wrong things, but we can only love that which is good. So we are told to do what we love to do and we will find that everything we need will come to us. Back we go to

emphasis on; "searching out truth" pure and simple.
Since all there is is God, the "kingdom of God" is
another way of saying "the Truth", or "what IS". As
our hearts and minds become accustomed to centering
our lives around the search for Truth; for seeing things
as they really are, our understanding of God opens.
Things go better and better for us in every way, and we
begin to see the realism in the Biblical saying "Try me
and see if I will not open the windows and pour forth
such a flood that there will not be room to receive it."

The difficulty in this world is, of course, learning to
tell the difference between truth and falsehood, which
masquerades so effectively and so often as truth. The
thing to realize is that we have to start somewhere,
and practice makes perfect. So we have to truly and
earnestly desire to know the truth about all things;
to seek it out actively and constantly, and things will
steadily improve. The simplest way to tell truth? Tell
the truth. Make it a habit.

It does indeed seem to us in this world, so accustomed
to disappointment, failure, sickness, and all the ills of
mortal mankind that something so simple and lovely

102

as God actually providing for our needs without strain and worry on our part, cannot possibly be true. But we are assured by those who seem to know, that it is indeed true. Isn't it worth checking out just as a hypothesis in case Jesus, for example, might have actually known what he was talking about? And in terms of having our needs met we would do well to ask ourselves how we got our bodies in the first place, along with such a fantastic place to put them. Not from a multinational corporation; that's for sure.

It is essential now that we come to understand these things. All the competitive, harmful things human beings do are done essentially out of fear; fear of not having enough of something; food, clothing, shelter, money, love, protection from harm, etc, etc, etc. How different things will be when we understand that we really <u>will</u> be provided for by That Which Created Us! The choice is between fear and faith. It couldn't be simpler but as prevailing thought patterns stand now on our planet, it could hardly be more difficult. The tide is so strong that it seems useless to buck it. Nonetheless, methinks it will soon be quite clear that we'd better give it a try. Difficult, shmifficult! We've driven a car on the moon.

3) What Death Isn't

We really need to get straight on the matter of death. We are so terrified of it that we can't bear even to think seriously about it; thus we allow it to keep right on terrifying us because we don't learn anything about it. What scares us so badly is the fact that it seems to us that when we die we become nothing, and the reason why that idea has such a grip on us is that we think we are our body, which for all practical purposes becomes nothing after we die. Yet something in us protests desperately "That will never happen to me!" Why? And why does that thought distress us so? Because deep within ourselves we know the truth; we know that we can never become nothing because there is no such thing as nothing and there is such a thing as us. That "us" can theoretically become anything else but obviously it can never become nothing.

We need to see what we are; what the "us" is that will continue after the death of our body. This really is not so hard to do when we just give it some attention; first we need to contemplate the fact that we so often refer to our body as "ours". We do this all the time but we seldom if ever spend any time examining what we mean by the "me" that owns "my" body, and the reason why we behave this way is, again, because we don't really see anything not solid as real. That must change, and it's a matter of practice. A simple exercise that can be very useful here is to imagine a purple pine tree, say ten feet tall and ten feet in front of you. While continuing to hold the image in your mind's eye (or, if you are a verbalist instead of a visualist, continuing to hold the sound of the words "purple pine tree" in your mind's ear), ask yourself who or what is holding that image (or sound). YOU are. This is what we are; we <u>are</u> that conscious being that lives our life; that takes in and processes information through the body and mind that God gave us, and that acts (gives out) in this world by expressing our desires through our body's mechanisms. We have to be able to <u>feel</u> ourselves in that way; it is entirely a matter of feeling. This conscious "you", by the way, is NOT created by your brain; your brain <u>registers</u> various aspects of your consciousness in order for them to be expressed through your body as you participate in the life of this world. That consciousness; that "you" is eternal.

Another way to realize the nature of your real self is to see yourself as that which awakens in the morning and says "By golly, here I am again in this amazing body, on this amazing ball in space, experiencing this amazing thing called 'life'". It is the same "you" that, when your body is inactive at night in this world, awakens in another world (state, plane, whatever) where you do many of the same things you do in this world during the waking state (and more); you walk, run, fly, think, talk; on and on. And when we die, this is the same self that will awaken in the next world, saying "By golly, here I am again, in <u>this</u> world!" So that's all death is; the putting off of the body, which is worn out due to our having cut ourselves off from the source of our being. This will not always be the case ("Even the last enemy, death, will be overcome"). But it is now absolutely essential that we come to understand the reality of what is not material; "the substance of things unseen". Until the real meaning and importance of this dawns on us we will remain trapped in the material world, unable to see beyond it to the infinitely greater realities that now beckon to us so powerfully. We must be able to see, not only with regard to the nature of the cosmos but of our own being as well, that by far the greater part of the iceberg is below the surface as it were, "unseen" but with real substance nonetheless.

4) Right and Wrong

It is vitally important that we get clear about the difference between Right and Wrong. Nineteenth and twentieth century philosophy seem to be able to do no better with this subject than to see it as a matter of individual opinion, but this is not only a useless way to look at it; it is terribly harmful to us because it leaves us with no compass, blundering around in a complex and difficult world with no solid moral center. We fail to realize that right is RIGHT and wrong is WRONG, and that this is absolutely not a matter of opinion but of cosmic law.

God made, as it were, a perfect harp upon which we play horrible music and then blame the harpmaker.

God made a perfect world; a perfect universe, a perfect cosmos. Part of that Creation is the human creature, which has (amazingly and very significantly) the ability to play bad music; to see things not as they are but as they are not, thus reaping the harvest of suffering that must come from wrongness. God has so arranged things that when we do right we experience pleasure and when we do wrong we experience pain; thus we must eventually, when the pain of wrongdoing becomes unbearable (as it is presently doing on this planet), wake up and fly right. Pain is God's NO sign; pleasure is God's YES sign. It's just that simple; the fact that pleasure and pain are so frequently mixed only means that right and wrong are frequently combined. But every shade of gray is made up of black and white and so it is with pleasure and pain; right and wrong. What a wonderful vision this presents us with! If we really are beginning to see this, then we can at last begin to do away with all suffering forever, by choosing to pursue rightness and to eschew wrongness. "Be ye perfect, even as your Father in Heaven is perfect." Practice makes perfect; shouldn't we get on with it?

I have to admit that I am baffled by the fact that we actually do go against the will of God; that we do wrong things. I can see why we have to have the ability do do so, because we are not marionettes; we are chips off the old block; creatures endowed, with respect to our individual worlds, with the same creative powers as our

Creator ("made in God's image"), and our destiny is to be creative on a scale that we can not as yet imagine. It is absolutely necessary that we have free will. But why we would actually <u>do</u> wrong eludes me. Why would we ever do something so stupid and harmful? Look at the sum total of pain that the human race (along with so many other creatures) has suffered over time; the mind reels. Right now this planet is filled with the groans of the sick, the tears of those in a nearly infinite variety of sorrow, the shrieks of the tortured and the maimed in war, and on and on and on. Why would we ever let ourselves in for such incalculable misery? I don't know. I wonder if we were so enchanted by this world that we let it capture our attention and got stuck in it, forgetting where we came from, thus becoming bewildered and desperate, but be that as it may, I am convinced that we are about to free ourselves at last from this dreadful state of affairs.

One thing that helps me to be patient in the face of such constant, stunning suffering goes back again to the law of conservation of energy which necessarily implies, among other things, that no creature can possibly be more powerful than That Which Created Everything; therefore God's plan MUST be fulfilled eventually (and how can we contemplate a flower, a child, or the grand drama of evolution without realizing that God has a plan; a reason for making all this happen?). So it's just a matter of time. Even if we trash this planet, we'll get another one if that's what we need; we got this one. Theoretically that could happen, but as a friend once observed, "It wouldn't be poetic!". We'll do ourselves a real favor if and when we wake up to the fact that we want everything to do with Right (Good) and nothing to do with Wrong (Evil). "Get thee behind me, Satan!"

Go with God's will (simple but not yet easy) and all the forces of Heaven and Earth will come to our assistance; continue to go against God's will and these forces will continue to appear to oppose us. They never actually oppose us, but like a train that runs us over because we insisted on lollygagging around on the tracks, it certainly appears to be working against us, in our ignorant and self-centered view of the matter (one of my brothers, when very young, really hit the bullseye on this one, saying through his tears "I stung myself on a wasp!"). This is why we come up with such ghastly notions as that of a "wrathful God". We do something wrong, we get slapped upside the head, and we think God punished us. GOD NEVER PUNISHES ANYONE. The most essential characteristic of God is love, and love does not punish. God simply put spikes at the end of every wrong-way tunnel, and we run up against those spikes with whatever speed we generated in our headlong rush in a wrong direction. Then we say God is punishing us. But what if God hadn't made Wrongness hurt? We'd then be able to go on forever making the same old mistakes. And we do indeed continue to make the same old mistakes; our capacity for pain would appear to be infinite. But it is not; sooner or later the pain of those mistakes must become unbearable because while the mistakes are the same as ever, the power with which we make them increases exponentially. A mistake repeated is a bigger mistake and it hurts more. So there's an easy way and a hard way. Go with God or go against God. But even if we decide to do the latter (which we certainly have) we can't keep on doing it forever because it will become too painful. And that is what's happening right now on this planet. And by the way, I believe that this is why Washington said "perhaps as <u>finally</u>" and Lincoln said "the <u>last</u>, best hope..."; both of these people were truly wise. They realized that mankind had always repeated the same basic mistakes; they also saw that we have done so with exponentially increasing power, and that therefore if we failed to correct these mistakes the time must come when things really hit the fan.

JESUS

I'm going to break in here because as I write, it's Christmas eve and I want to talk about Jesus.

I'm one of those people who at one time or another during the holidays feel sad. There are a number of different explanations for this feeling but I know exactly why I feel that way; it is because of what is being missed. The winter theme, the Christmas spirit, the tree, the music, the giving of gifts, the family gatherings, the snow, all these things are wonderful. But where is the focus on the central meaning of this major celebration? How often do we hear anywhere but in church (and how strongly do we hear it even there?) any deep thought about the stunning power, beauty, and promise of Jesus's message? Let me set forth what it is that I believe Jesus was trying to tell us:

Do not worship him, he said; worship God, by following Jesus's instructions and becoming like him. He explicitly told us "The Kingdom of Heaven is within you", and "These things and more shall ye do". I take this to mean that Jesus saw himself as no different from any of us except that he realized more fully than we do what he really was (and what we are too; he asked "Why do you call <u>me</u> holy?"). He told us a great deal about how to seek out these truths and also about what we could expect to find if and when we sincerely seek, and he realized that it is our common destiny to enter these realms of being. He was trying to tell us that we only see the tip of the iceberg of our own being or of the rest of existence but that it was our destiny to expand our view and to experience the as yet unimaginable joy that comes with this awakening.

But it is up to each of us to choose to awaken; to learn, to grow, and thus to achieve our destiny. Books, teaching of all kinds, are wonderful but it is up to each of us to look within ourselves to discover what the Kingdom of Heaven really is. Only when we do this can we understand what the books and teachers were talking about.

What more wonderful message could there be for suffering mankind? Yet we seldom seem to pay much attention to it. "Too good to be true" seems to be the general reaction to such radiant promises, but let me say that (within cosmic law) anything is possible and nothing is too good to be true. We need so badly to raise our sights; to realize that ideals are what attract us toward our destiny; they guide us forward. We should form the highest ideals we can imagine and then work to build them into our everyday lives rather than deafly, dumbly, and blindly accepting such dreadful notions as "too good to be true". "That's life" we say, and indeed it is, but that should be the beginning of the discussion, not the end. The question should be "How can we change it?"

And another thing; forget the odds. At the moment things have deteriorated so badly; so much power has gone to the corporations, and they have such a lock on Congress and the media, that it seems impossible to turn things around. No, it is not impossible. It will take effort and greatly increased understanding to generate the necessary energy, but it certainly is possible. And we should not forget; as we do God's will, God will provide; new things will come along that we never could have predicted, and that from our present standpoint would seem to be miraculous. After all, how likely would anyone in 1929 have considered a weekend jaunt on the moon? If it takes miracles, I'm expecting miracles. And obviously, a "miracle" isn't something that can't happen; it's just something that does happen that we don't understand until we look back at it.

For far too long we have crawled about on the surface of this planet like miserable sinners, lowly worms, and so on. We are indeed sinners ("sin", by the way, comes from a Greek word that simply means "to miss the mark"; there is no connotation whatever of "yucky you" for doing so); that is our problem in a nutshell.

Why should anything prevent us from seeking out the solution to that problem? The message is simply "We get what we pay for", or "You can't have your cake and eat it too". We need so badly to awaken to the simple fact that if we go against God's will (sin) we must reap a harvest of pain. But when we strive to live in accordance with God's will (goodness) then we must reap a harvest of pleasure. When we go against God's will we put ourselves in opposition to all that is good, and all the forces of Heaven and earth seem to be working against us but when we consciously attempt to do good, we are cooperating with God's will and all the forces of nature work with us, as they were designed to do. There is no such thing as a Wrathful God; God never punishes anyone. The central characteristic of God is Love. Don't blame the Rolls-Royce if you drive it into the ditch.

There is another tremendously important thing to realize in all this in connection with the question of freedom and right living. If we each are free to form our own opinions about everything, and to do whatever we choose, how can we expect anything but anarchy and chaos as a result? In fact, don't we have something close to that right now, and could that not be ascribed (as it often seems to be, explicitly or implicitly) to an excess of freedom? No, it is not an excess of freedom that is the problem; it is the <u>irresponsible use of freedom</u>. It is now absolutely essential that we realize that freedom and responsibility are the two sides of one coin; they cannot be separated successfully, regardless of how hard we try to pretend otherwise.

We must also realize that opinions are far more a beginning than an end; they are only a step on the way to the realization of truth. But if we persist in our search for truth we find it, and opinion evolves into certainty. Is it not then obvious that as each of us does discover the truth about things, we must come more and more into agreement with each other? And does it not follow that eventually we must become fully in agreement when we have truly realized how it is with things, because things are precisely what they are; no more and no less?

What then lies before us is simply this: doing good things and not doing bad things, which is another way of saying "doing the will of God". We are free to do whatever we please, but until we desire to do only good we cannot achieve our destiny. That is why the Bible speaks of "(God), in whose service is perfect freedom". And how can we assign any limit to the possibilities of a future where all is well; where only goodness exists? Things in such a state can only work together to build new and wonderful realities, because there will be no negative forces at work; no conflict, no fear, nothing like that at all. Is that not, in Shakespeare's words, "a consummation devoutly to be wished"?

Can we not see the immense promise and glory of Jesus's message? He tells us that our future is assured; that it is very much more wonderful than we have dared to even imagine. He said that ALL pain of any kind would disappear forever, as we become completely good ("Be ye perfect, even as your Father in heaven is perfect"). He said that we are all children of God; members of the human family, and that the key word in life is "Love". If we realized this, he said, we would grow into the same life that he had already realized, and he said that we WILL do this. This to me is the meaning of Christmas; what this master soul was trying to show us. He stands ahead of us on the road of life, beckoning to us and showing us the way.

THE FOUR GREAT QUESTIONS

Here's some more of what we can expect to awaken to as we turn in the right direction and our awareness grows: I'm particularly fond of this exercise because it deals with the virtually infinite complexity of creation and shows how utterly simple it is in essence. Each of the Four Great Questions has the same answer, and that answer boils down to a single word; God. Here's the deal:

First Question: What Am I?

Almost all of us take ourselves fundamentally to be our body. We associate ourselves with our names, and we associate our names with our bodies, as when we say "John and Mary went to the movies". We know that our bodies die and for all practical purposes become nothing, and since we think we <u>are</u> that body, death would necessarily seem to mean that we become nothing when we die. This thought frightens us so much that we generally don't even want to hear about death, let alone think about it, as a result of which we don't learn anything about it. This is fascinating when you do think about it, for two reasons. First, if we were to become nothing then we wouldn't care, because we wouldn't exist, so what's the fuss about? But also, one thing of which we can be certain is that we can never become nothing because we are something and there is no such thing as nothing (the law of conservation of energy again). So the case that we normally make to ourselves against death is not only entirely negative, it's on a fairly low level of rationality.

I believe that our confusion in this matter comes largely from the tension between our idea of death as we normally interpret it and our deeper self calling out to us the truth, which is that what we really are can never die. Confusing indeed; we have a deep inner feeling that "That can't happen to me", but we don't know how to relate that feeling to our normal life so we push it away and continue to fear something that could never happen.

We are ever so much more than our bodies, but for the moment let's pretend that our body is the essence of our being. Then the question becomes "What is our body?" Our body is one of the forms of matter that has evolved on this planet; if we want to know what it is we need to see what it has always been; to trace its evolution back as far as we can.

We can take a giant step right away by realizing that our bodies, like every other form of matter on earth, are made of whatever we wish to call the primordial state of matter that constituted the earth before it became differentiated into the many forms with which we are familiar. We know that our planet was entirely molten before it cooled, crusted, and began the astonishing combination of processes whereby that crust assumed the different forms which related to each other in all the fascinating ways that we call the history of our planet. In that early stage in which the earth's crust formed, there were no vegetables, animals, or anything else but rock, which consisted of cooling lava. Beneath its crust the earth is still molten, and we can still see that primordial matter (lava) coming to the surface in many places, cooling, hardening, and forming what we call rock. When the original rock had formed it then went through the processes that we are familiar with and which we call evolution. This evolution has been marked by three major shifts in the character of forms which matter has taken, as the mineral form evolved into vegetable form, then into animal form, and then into homo sapiens. As we have observed, we are now in the early stages of the next major change.

But if we seek to know what we are by tracing back the nature of what we came from, we need to keep going if we are to see what we really are at base. So we must realize that before any of the above processes happened; before the earth formed as a molten ball in space, it had a substantial history already. Our current knowledge of what matter was before it became that ball takes us back to what we call the Big Bang, which is the closest we have yet been able to come to what we could call the origin of creation as we know it. Those who deal with what came before the big bang (the mystics, not the scientists) point out that no matter how far back you go with a material analysis you must always be faced with the unknown that lies beyond whatever point you have reached (something like the ball that can never hit the wall because it's always halving the distance between it and the wall), and that this is the limit of the scientific method to yield truth. But the point that the mystics focus on here is that since something cannot come from nothing, all things must have been caused to do whatever they did by whatever made everything happen, and that is God. So if you trace our bodies back all the way, as it were, you unavoidably get to the source of all things, which is not only the creator of the forms of creation but also the very essence of each form, because as we have observed, when God began to create all things, all God could have had to make anything out of was God; there was nothing else. There is nothing else, and there can never be anything but God. Each form of matter is a form of God; God <u>being</u> that thing. So if we go back to our material origins we find that our bodies are, like all material forms, not really material at all but spiritual. This is what our science has shown us by pointing out that matter is not solid. Let's apply this approach to the question of what our bodies are, working in the present instead of the past.

Our bodies are forms of matter. All forms of matter turn out to be not solid, which is to say, not single entities at all but communities composed of a huge number of different material entities, which our science first identified as molecules. These guys are very small compared to the body that they make up but lo and behold, each molecule is not a single entity either but is itself a community composed of a huge number of entities that we call atoms. And guess what, the atoms aren't single entities either; they're made up of sub-atomic particles, which are themselves composed of strings, then quarks, and now our scientists are at the point where they hardly know what words to use to describe what they're looking at, because they're no longer looking at many things; they're looking at one thing; that of which all things are made. As Sir James Jeans, one of the great early physicists, perceptively observed: "The universe begins to look more like a vast thought than a vast machine."

No more valuable truth has ever been or could be revealed by science than that essential, non-material oneness of all material things. Can we see that, just as with our going back in time, when we go deeply enough into the present we find the same thing; the oneness of all things? All creation is not just created by God (history) but composed of God as well, in the present. So whether you trace our physical form back in time or analyze it in the present, you end up with the realization that what it is, is God. All things are forms of God (which is why it can be said that if you know anything about anything, you know something about everything). So even if we define ourselves as "just" our body we see, if we look, that in essence we are God.

But now let's take into account the fact that we really are not our bodies any more than we are our cars, our houses, or any other vehicle in which we ride through life; they are ours. We have dealt with this already; we see that our real self lies beneath the surface, as it were, and just as with an iceberg, the vastly greater part of that self is unseen, which ultimately means spiritual. Not only does it have the "substance of things unseen", it is in fact far more substantial than the evanescent form that we perceive as our body and which we assume will at some point cease to maintain that form (die). We have already analyzed this matter; we can cut to the chase for our present purpose by realizing that all of creation, whether material or non-material, must have come from the same source and must be composed of the same thing at base. And that thing is God.

So when we ask what we are, whether we take up the question historically or in the present, materially or spiritually, we come inescapably to the conclusion that we are forms of God.

Second Question: Where Do I Come From?

We have already answered this question; when we see that no matter how we define ourselves, we must have come from and must be composed of God, we have the answer.

Third Question: Where Am I Going?

To the same "place" we came from. Since there is nothing but God, there can be no "place" to go to that is not created by and composed of God. We were originally "in" God, we are still "in" God, and we will always be "in" God. Like the prodigal son, we have the illusion of having left our Father's house only because we dreamed ourselves away from full awareness of God by locking ourselves into the space-time continuum. We now have to break out of that limited state and go back to the garden, as it were. That is our journey; "where we're going". And we're getting very close to that blessed return. So where are we going? (Back) to God.

Fourth Question: What's Going On?

There is a great Dream going on. "Dream" is the only word that I can think of that adequately conveys the deepest meaning of the fact that matter is not solid. Whether we speak of Sir James Jeans's "vast thought" or of a "dream" we are speaking of phenomena of consciousness, and that is what's happening with all of creation; a vast happening in the consciousness of That Which Created All Things, or God. We are "chips off the old block"; we have been endowed by our Creator with bodies, minds, and souls (individual consciousness), through which we can do, within the limits of cosmic law, anything we choose to do. (You want to ramble around on the moon? Go ahead! You want to tear each other to pieces? You can do that too.) Somehow we separated ourself from our original awareness of oneness with God and got locked into the space-time continuum, seeing only the forms within that continuum and excluding from our consciousness the rest of the iceberg; the far more significant eternal and infinite essence of all things. Our journey is that represented by the story of the prodigal son; returning home from our wandering, there to find that it will be as though we had never left, except that we will have the benefit of what we have learned from our journey. That is the nature of our life, our destiny. That's what's going on, and all within the One consciousness that is God.

So we see that each of these questions has the same answer, when they are thought through; God. When we really understand that there never was anything but God, there is nothing but God, and there can never be anything but God, we have the key to all four of the Great Questions. And it is toward that state of awareness that we are rapidly moving; what we have to look forward to. When we've worked through the turmoil of this birth into the Fifth Kingdom, we will find ourselves in a state of being of which we have scarcely allowed ourselves to dream.

CONCLUSION

Brothers and sisters, it comes down to this: there is a choice that we are forcing ourselves to make. Now is the time. The wheel of evolution has turned; it continues to manifest God's plan (we thought it would stop?). We can continue to go against that plan (willingly do bad things) or to go with it (willingly do good things). A substantial part of our foreseeable future depends upon which choice we make.

It was inevitable that this time would come. Humanity has always behaved just like the other animals, giving top priority to individual needs and desires or to the needs and desires of whatever group they felt most closely associated with. Thus as individuals and as groups, we have always been in competition with each other; we have always been at war with each other. And we have done so with constantly increasing power. It is self-evident that under such conditions a point must eventually come where we have so much power that its continued use in the usual ways will destroy the very things that we think we are protecting. We reached that point with the invention of the atomic bomb; now, in a general nuclear exchange, we will destroy civilization as we know it, and there are few among us who would say that that would be worthwhile. So we must now choose to behave differently.

It has to be emphasized that if we do not rise to the occasion, if we fail to make the right choices now, if we simply cannot bring ourselves to face facts that are becoming undeniable, then we must expect truly dreadful consequences. Things will be as bad as they would have been good had we done the right thing. Bob Dylan astutely observed that "he who is not busy being born is busy dying." If we do not get better, we do not stand still; we get worse, and at the rate things are going, that can only mean <u>much</u> worse. The "good Germans" during World War II were not demonstrating characteristics unique to Germans; they were showing us what happens when ordinary human beings abdicate their ordinary human responsibilities, as most of us are so prone to do. I have to predict that if we fail to face the all-important challenge that now confronts us, then something terribly similar to what happened with Hitler may well happen here. The shocking split that currently divides us between "liberal" and "conservative" views will grow. The influence of short-sighted, spiritually ignorant, heartless self-interest will increase even beyond the level of control that it now possesses. Intolerance will reach horrifying levels. Anyone with a dissenting view from the official norm will be persecuted (of course, they already are in many ways); official repression could become fully Orwellian. With the restrictions on our fundamental freedoms that we have, in our fear and sloth, allowed to degrade our nation since 9/11 through the likes of the Patriot Act and the National Defense Authorization Act, we are well on the way already on that downward path. We should think with the utmost care about the reality of the choice that we now face in terms of our individual and collective behavior, and about the seriousness of the consequences that must result from that choice. Which of course means that we should also deeply contemplate how wonderful the results will be if and when we muster the strength and courage to choose rightly.

Some very intelligent people contend that we have gone too far; that it is now impossible to avoid going over the cliff into disaster, which could involve the destruction of life as we know it on this planet. If we consult only our minds, we have to accept the fact that this is a rational possibility, backed up by an enormous amount of facts. We certainly do have the capacity to heedlessly hurl ourselves over that cliff. Will we do so or will we come to our senses? It's up to us; the choice is ours.

But is it not self-evident that if we go on the assumption that it's completely hopeless we'll see no reason to do what's necessary to save ourselves and that we will thus guarantee the continuation of what we deplore? Is it not equally obvious that so long as there is a chance of success, however remote, there is reason for hope and action? If the bomb is an inch from the ground it is in that inch that we have to work, and with God's help who knows what inspirations will present themselves as we genuinely confront our problems instead of ignoring or denying them? Remember, the odds mean nothing. What are the odds of our being here in the first place? That having been said, I would respectfully suggest that with the bomb as close to the ground as it now would seem to be, we had better get going.

One very important thing to realize is that even if we were to go over the cliff and destroy our planet, that would absolutely not be the end of the human journey, although it would surely be a major setback. We'd get a new planet if that was appropriate and we'd proceed as best we could. But I do not believe that this is what's going to happen. I think that enough of us will awaken in time to what's really going on, that we will learn to consult our hearts above our minds, that we'll achieve the critical mass which will allow us to do what needs to be done, and that we'll be OK. Much better than just OK in fact, because then we'll be cooperating with God instead of opposing God, and all the resources of heaven and earth will rush to our assistance. I find that a situation to look forward to very eagerly indeed. The human race has been looking "through a glass darkly";

now we must look through a glass clearly. We <u>can</u> do this: we can strip away our illusions and see things as they really are.

One of the most crippling fantasies we have allowed ourselves to accept is the notion that things must always continue to be the way they have always been. "It's human nature", we say, "to do both evil and good; right and wrong. There never was a time when our behavior was not a mixture of the two and there never will be." Says who? All "human nature" means is what human beings have the capacity to do; one of the things we can do is to choose between right and wrong and thus turn suffering into joy.

We often hear it said that suffering is good; that we need it because of what we learn from it. But what is it that we learn? In every case, it is what <u>not</u> to do. When we stop doing wrong things we will cease to suffer. We have been allowing ourselves to accept all manner of wrong things; we have exercised an enormous variety of harmful capacities, for reasons we have discussed above; primarily out of fear. The greatest figures in our history have always told us that we can and must eventually choose which of our abilities we will use and which we simply will not use. We must become <u>responsible</u> creatures. We must will to do good, and good only. When we awaken and make this conscious choice as free individuals, history will speak quite differently of human nature.

We must come to understand that our individual life consists of infinitely more than just the life of our body. Far, far from being meaningless, that life is meaningful beyond our ability to even imagine at this time, but our ability to understand what that meaning consists of, together with our interest in doing so will grow, at a speed directly proportional to our desire for that to happen. We have a future; a glorious and infinite future that we all share, and we are soon to realize that we do not have to leave this world to discover that and to increase our understanding of that future and of all that is connected with it. We will come to understand that that is what we've been here for all along.

We in the United States of America are uniquely positioned to lead the way in the astonishing adventure that is now before us all. We have a remarkable combination of resources that make that task relatively easy compared to the situation in many other places. Our "melting pot" has shown that people of any race, nationality, or any other thing that commonly sets us apart from one another can live perfectly well together. We demonstrate this at every traffic light, where human beings of every stripe agree to cooperate with astonishing precision. We do so for one obvious reason; we see that we have no choice. And so it is now with the entirety of human existence on this planet; we have no choice but to behave well if we expect to continue to live here. We will soon be unable to deny that fact.

We can and will realize that the similarities that unite us are infinitely more significant than the differences that keep us apart. We will realize that our highest personal interest is the common interest. We will turn toward each other in appreciation of each other's strengths rather than turning away from each other in fear of each other's weaknesses. We will come to see that it is absolutely in our best interest to see (admit rather than deny) what we are doing wrong, to think clearly about it, to correct it, and to enjoy the results of so doing. These results will be infinitely greater than just a stable economy for the indefinite future. As I hope I have adequately indicated, they will be of an order that we have not as yet dared even to imagine. Together we can and will do what must be done. Together we will share life as the single human family we always were. Together we will achieve our destiny; we will go with God, into a whole new world. Just you wait and see.